Adrian Deans

Adrian Deans is the author of three richly praised previous novels: *Straight Jacket, Mr Cleansheets* and *THEM*. He is a lawyer, journalist and novelist. He lives at Avoca Beach with his wife, Karen.

For Christine and Kazzie

POLITICAL FOOTBALL
Lawrie McKinna's Dangerous Truth

as told to

Adrian Deans

High Horse

Distributed by Dennis Jones and Associates
Unit 1/10 Melrich Road, Bayswater, Victoria 3153, Australia
www.dennisjones.com.au

National Library of Australia
Cataloguing-in-Publication data:

Deans, Adrian, author.
McKinna, Lawrie, author.

Political football: Lawrie McKinna's dangerous truth /
Adrian Deans, Lawrie McKinna.

ISBN: 9780646958385 (paperback)

Subjects: McKinna, Lawrie.
Soccer players-Australia-Biography.
Soccer coaches-Australia-Biography.
Mayors-New South Wales-Gosford-Biography.
Politicians-Australia-Biography.
Scottish Australians-Biography.

796.334092

Published in 2016 by High Horse Books
Cover design: Lucy Barker, *www.lucybarker.com.au*

Praise for *Political Football*

As readable as Lawrie is gregarious, which is very. High on brogue and yarns and very low on political correctness. I wasnae sure what to expect with Lawrie's book, but he didnae disappoint

— Andy Harper, Fox Sports

You would be hard pressed to invent Lawrie McKinna's life story: from journeyman footballer in Scotland to coach of the year in the A-League in Australia and Mayor of Gosford. Perhaps only a novelist who knows his football could weave a convincing story of McKinna's picaresque career as Adrian Deans has done. I read it in five hours flat and could not put it down.

— Roy Hay, *History of Football in Australia: A Game of Two Halves* (with Bill Murray)

Lawrie McKinna is an important figure in Australian Football and Adrian Deans tells his story in a compelling and mesmerising fashion.

— Con Stamocostas, *afootballstory*

Grab your drink of choice, sit down and start reading. It will feel like you are listening to Lawrie telling stories of his life in your own living room — and it's an amazing journey. Lawrie McKinna is one of the most likeable guys in football — a man who has made the most of his talents and is not afraid to have a laugh along the way. That may well be the secret of his success in the murky worlds of football and politics.

— Ashley Morrison, broadcaster and author

Contents

Foreword by Alex Tobin ix

McCult of Personality x

1 How Blue was My Valley 1

2 A Poacher's Instinct 9

3 Hullo, Hullo, we are the Billy Boys 18

4 'Do You Want to be a Professional Footballer, Son?' 25

5 The Magic of the Cup 40

6 The Road to Wembley 53

7 Power, Passion and Pain 63

8 One Door Closes … 73

9 Thieves and Billionaires 85

10 Heaven and Hell 96

11 The Agony and the Ecstasy and the Agony 111

12 The Extra Mile 131

13 May You be Fated to Live in Interesting Times 146

14 Changes in the Land Where Nothing Ever Happened 160

15 Reflections and Projections: The Dangerous Truth 172

From Lawrie's Mates: Tributes & Reflections 180

Playing and Coaching Record 193

Foreword

Lawrie McKinna is a man of the people — gregarious and social to a fault. Who else but Lawrie could have morphed from an A League coach, to a council mayor, to an A League CEO within a few short years; dedicated to the game he loves and possessing the innate ability to work and engage with others in a team environment.

It has been my pleasure to know Lawrie for decades and to have worked with him for many of those years out on the training field and on match days. In addition to this we have shared endless cups of coffee discussing football, business, politics, family, history, Scotland and more football.

Despite working successfully in a variety of very senior positions Lawrie has never taken himself too seriously. Evidence of this was when discussing what this this foreword should look like, Lawrie just said: 'Don't be afraid to take the piss out of me'.

On that note I might mention a certain overseas football tour trip that Lawrie put together some years ago during the gap between the NSL ending and the A League beginning. A tour clear in my memory as it was the last tour I had as a professional player. Lawrie put in an enormous amount of work and detail to organise a team from scratch incorporating professional NSL players from Victoria and NSW. Organising the team with all those separate contractual arrangements was a mammoth effort. On top of that was the logistics of a trip to China and all that involved. It was an absolute triumph of careful, painstaking management with every detail covered … except his own expired passport.

We had the trip of a lifetime without him!

Great memories always. Thanks Lawrie.

Alex Tobin
Socceroos captain & NSL record holder

McCult of Personality

Australians have always loved the Scots.

There's something about a broad, Scottish accent that puts a grin on our faces. We think there's a joke coming because the sound of the accent is somehow funny — 'jock-ular' perhaps? Billy Connolly wouldn't have been half as funny if he'd been a Kiwi: 'Git us a Bovril, eh bro.'

Lawrie McKinna is the quintessential 'jock-ular' Scot — big, loud, funny and knows his way round a football pitch. But in a game of such tribal loves and hatreds, Lawrie is one of the few characters universally admired. Obviously, that accent gives him an unfair advantage but in Lawrie's case there's more. He is a connector — a genuine 'Man of the People' as the following incident illustrates.

Shortly before the A-League commenced, I had moved from Sydney to Avoca Beach. This meant that I felt honour-bound to support the Mariners, even though I had a natural affinity for Sydney (where most of my friends and family still lived). Sydney were therefore my secret second team, and I was perfectly happy to support both, except when they played each other. In those games I supported the Mariners, but every goal was like a dagger through my heart.

On one such occasion, when Sydney were visiting the Coast, I was standing discreetly with some Sydney mates at the back of the Cove when suddenly a voice booms in my ear: 'Adrian! What are you doing with this lot?'

Lawrie had recently transitioned from coaching to General Manager of Football and always visited the away fans to say g'day. I started to introduce him to my mates but, as soon as the crowd realised who was in their midst, the most curious transformation happened. The match was suddenly forgotten for the fifty-odd people in closest proximity who gathered round to shake his hand, pat him on the back and listen to that accent as Lawrie held court at the back of Bay 31 for five minutes or so.

And these weren't just any Sydney fans. This was The Cove — sky blue fanatics who detest everything north of the Hawkesbury and refer to the Mariners as Sea Bogans. In Cove-ite eyes, Lawrie was a Sea Bogan chieftain, worthy only of hatred and contempt, yet such was the force of his charm they fell before him like cougars at George Clooney's birthday party. If Kevin Muscat had pulled a stunt like that they'd have torn him arsehole to breakfast.

It was also an insight into the cult of personality which transformed politics in the twentieth century. Lawrie's charm and popularity would be a godsend to any political party, so it is no wonder he was heavily courted by both sides of the Australian political spectrum before being elected to local government as an independent, and has now done four years as mayor of Gosford.

Football and politics — player, coach and mayor — but in listening to Lawrie's stories there's a dimension that can only be conveyed in his Kilmarnock accent. That's why I've tried to give just a little of his aural flavour with some phonetic spelling.

Even though ahm no Scoatish masel.

Adrian Deans
Avoca Beach
June 2016

P.S. Come on Bozza. Come on Warnie — I'll do you guys as well!

1

How Blue Was My Valley

The Chinese have an ancient curse: 'May you be fated to live in interesting times.'

On face value, it doesn't sound like much of a curse — better to live in interesting times than boring times, right? Wrong. Interesting times are those written about by historians because they involve war, revolution, plague, famine, earthquakes or a thousand other perils to disturb the peace and tranquillity of human life.

In football terms, Lawrie McKinna has lived in interesting times. Growing up and learning the game in sectarian Scotland, emigrating to Australia to play and coach in the equally political National Soccer League, coaching in the A-League and even in China where the multi-layered subtleties of politics, family ties and business look more like rampant corruption to simplistic western minds.

But Lawrie hasn't just survived — he has thrived despite being blessed with only modest talent. Lawrie is one of those people determined to do the best with what he has, and the results of his efforts are chronicled in the pages that follow.

Lawrie McKinna was born on 8 July 1961 in the village of Galston on the outskirts of Kilmarnock in Ayrshire, Scotland. First son of Lawrence (senior) and Jessie McKinna, he was only in Scotland for two years before the family emigrated, temporarily as it turned out, to Australia.

When you consider that my accent is one of my distinguishing features (in Australia, at least), it is both ironic and somehow fitting that I started life speaking with an Aussie accent.

True.

When I was only two the family came out to Australia for about three years, but those were the years I was learning to talk — so by the time we got back to Scotland in '66 I sounded more like Paul Hogan than Billy Connolly. All the girls at the primary school would chase me around the playground begging me to talk Aussie at them. But no-one could understand me! I had to have elocution lessons in Kilmarnock to scrub the Aussie out so I could communicate with my peers.

Galston is one of those small villages in Scotland on the edge of a larger town. It was one of several villages that made up The Valley — with still a few farms about but rapidly becoming industrialised. There're not so many jobs in town these days but back then most people worked in the lace factories, small shops or the various public services. Dad was a bus driver — the most popular driver in town. He had the gift of the gab so strong that people used to catch his bus even when they had to go somewhere else! Dad wisnae bothered, he'd still drop the old wifies off where they needed to go.

If we'd known it, we were poor, but life was pretty good despite my so-called humble beginnings. In terms of living in a big house with rich parents and having only the finest things and going to a posh school … aye, humble beginnings. But I saw it as a world of privilege — nothing to do but play football in the street with my mates and no future but the dole or the factory unless you could kick a ball straight. I wanted to be a footballer so living in a nice house and going to a posh school would have been a serious handicap.

I remember telling my mother on my first day of primary school that I was gaunny play for Rangers one day and buy her a Hillman Avenger. I was gaunny be paid £100 a a week and she could have £95. Clearly I was not much interested in money, which is just as well, as I couldnae have played at the highest level in Scotland and Australia if money was important.

One of my earliest memories is running to school with my football — rain, hail or snow. I'd be passing the ball off walls, lamp posts, trees, the kerb, and running for the rebound. Then I'd get to school, play football for an hour before class, run home again at lunchtime. Have my lunch and then back to school — always with the football glued to my boot like Ginger Tompkins on the Benny Hill Show.

Games at school tended to be on hard asphalt, or on cow paddocks. It was Housing Estate versus Housing Estate, and we'd pinch strawberry nets from the local market gardens to make nets for the goals. It certainly added to the authenticity when you could beat your marker, go round a heifer, dodge a pile of steaming shite and slam your shot through a strawberry net. Just like Denis Law getting the winner at Hampden against the Auld Enemy.

My first proper organised game was for Galston Primary when I was 11, at West End Park. I played centre-half and I scored, as I would often do in my future career, with my head from a corner. I can still remember that ball flying at me and it just seemed the most natural thing in the world to turn my forehead towards the goal as the ball arrived and somehow the ball flew off my noggin into the roof of the net. No-one ever taught me that — the right technique for heading at goal — it's just something I had naturally.

Almost the only thing, because I should say from the very start that I was never a gifted footballer. Aye, I loved the game and played it obsessively, but so did every other boy in Scotland and most of them had a lot more talent than Lawrie McKinna. I never once made any sort of representative side and struggled even to make the year side at High School. But I did eventually make the side because that's the one thing that set me apart from most of my peers — determination. I desperately wanted to make the side so a mere lack of talent wisnae gaunny stop me. I trained hard, played to my strengths, and did whatever I had to do.

I spent hours kicking a ball against a wall, always trying to hit the same spot to improve my passing and shooting. Then I'd keep the ball up by heading against the wall. You need to develop tremendous neck muscles and snappy technique to manage that and by the time I was playing professionally heading the ball with power was an important part of my game — but I'll get to that later.

About that time I started in the Boys Brigade team. The Boys Brigade were sort of like the Scouts — only more football and less playing with our toggles. The only drawback was that you had to attend church in order to play, so every Sunday I'd maintain my eligibility by listening to how Jesus had died for our sins and how he didnae want us to follow Celtic. But it meant I got to play for a regular side and received my first professional wages, because when we won the end of season Cup we took it round all the eight pubs in the village and the punters used to fill the Cup with spare change to be shared by the wee victors.

Anyway, I started attending Loudon Academy (High School) which was named after Loudon Hill, where Robert the Bruce trounced the English in 1307 and where young Scots have been trouncing English ever since. Loudon Academy took all the protestant kids from The Valley. The Valley was Galston, Darvel, Newmilns and Hurlford — not far from Kilmarnock, where all the Catholic kids went. That's when we first started to encounter sectarian segregation. The conversation at our dinner table after the first day of High School was probably typical:

> *Lawrie Junior:* Where's Patrick? How's he no at ma school?'
> *Lawrie Senior:* He goes tae the Catholic school.
> *Lawrie Junior:* What are Catholics?
> *Lawrie Senior:* Dinnae worry about Catholics. They're different.

So there you go, a perfectly adequate explanation for the centuries-old sectarian divide, but it's just as well. I didnae really know who the Catholics were so I couldnae hate them like I was supposed to.

At High School the Sports Master was Jim McFadzean — a local football legend who'd played for Ayr United and Kilmarnock. He saw something in me (probably my size and potential for violence) and encouraged me to try out for some of the better local club sides. I was unsuccessful at Kilmarnock Boys Club but was selected (with a couple of my pals) to play for Belfield Red Lions. It was always two buses and a walk to where we'd get picked up and driven off to play on yet another cow paddock. More often than not these games were just a huge mud bath where everyone steams in and kicks lumps out of each other. The only decent surfaces were the all-weather red blaze pitches we played on in Glasgow.

Belfield Red Lions could also be regarded as a semi-pro outfit because the coach used to give us pontoon tickets to sell to pay for our bus fares to games. Pontoon tickets were a bit like scratch lottery tickets so it's basically gambling, but no-one minded children being involved

Above: With my parents in Australia. Note the Quonset huts in the background.

Left: On the set of a Disney movie with my sister. I was playing Pinocchio.

5

Like Ginger Tomkins I always had the ball glued to my boot and my brother Andrew was at least 3 before he could get it off me.

Back home to Scotland. I'm third from right in the back row and still had an Aussie accent at this time.

in black market gambling operations — not in those days. We live in a fuckin' nanny state now.

Despite the fact I didnae really hate Catholics, there were always fights when we played them. Possibly because our goalkeeper Bruce McNaught was as lippy as keepers tend to be and couldnae help himself. 'Watch the papes!' he'd shout as we prepared to face a corner. 'Fenian scum at twelve o'clock!' he'd scream as the ball was swung over, and if the referee was a mason he'd get away with it. If the ref was a Catholic he'd find a reason to give a penalty, but either way the game would end in a brawl and I'd come home with multiple wounds that were never discovered until the mud was washed away in the bathroom sink.

•   •   •

About this time my enthusiasm for Glasgow Rangers developed into a deep and abiding adoration. I used to go occasionally to Ibrox with my mate Jim White and his dad, Harry, but I never went to an Old Firm match until I was 12. My mother didnae want us to go, especially so soon after the Ibrox Disaster of 1971 (in which 66 people had died), but with a couple of pals I jumped onto the Valley supporters' bus and this time it was completely different. This time there were flags and banners and the singing of secret songs. The atmosphere on the bus was intense, unlike any previous journey, and I understood that I was about to be admitted to a very special mystery and brotherhood.

When we got to the ground the singing had changed. The words were no longer secret — they were all about age-old grievances, bitter hatred and vengeance. I got stuck into it with gusto, singing my heart out like all my mates. From that time we were confirmed Rangers die-hards and revelling in the emotion, colour and glorious bigotry.

Funnily enough, I don't remember anything about the game — just the life changing, soul-consuming atmosphere and drama on the terraces.

Back home in The Valley, my mother was extremely upset when she found out where I'd been, but dad was nae bothered. He was never much focused on football himself as he was so preoccupied with his family provider responsibilities, because besides being the bus driver he was also the local poacher — but more on that later.

• • •

Despite enjoying the Rangers songs, I suppose it goes to show that I never really absorbed the sectarian agenda when you consider I was just as happy to play with the Catholics as against them. In my teenage years I occasionally played for the Catholic Youth Club, mainly because I didnae have to go to church to be eligible.

One of the lads from the local Catholic school was Steve Nicol who, like me, emigrated to Australia and these days practises as a doctor in Berkley Vale, not far from where I live. Steve is therefore my doctor and we get along quite famously — reminiscing about the past as we discuss my health. He's a very thorough practitioner, insisting that I have all the tests that a man of my vintage ought to be having on a regular basis — especially the digital examination to check for prostate cancer. I've no problem with that, but I do have a question. Can you explain to me, Dr Nicol, why it is so important when I'm bent over your table with my breeks about my ankles that you must administer the test wearing your Celtic scarf?

2

A Poacher's Instinct

Life in semi-rural Scotland back in the 60s and 70s could be pretty rough. It was sometimes a matter of life and death and young Lawrie often had to make snap decisions …

The car screeched to a sudden halt and a rifle was pressed against my face.

'Dinnae you move.'

I couldnae breathe and I couldnae watch. I closed my eyes in anticipation of the shot, and then blam!

'Got the bastard!'

I leapt immediately from my dad's mini van and bolted into the field where a rabbit was rolling in the grass. If it was still twitching when I got there I'd have to snap its neck but it meant the McKinna's were eating meat — or maybe selling it on the sly to the local butchers or my dad's large network of private customers.

As the eldest son of the village poacher, my duties were privileged in comparison with my younger siblings. I got to ride out at night with dad, fetch the carcases (applying the *coup de grace* as necessary) and sling them in the back of the van. I was also in charge of marketing and security, but my younger siblings (Andrew and Angela) were on skinning and gutting detail, which I didnae fancy at all.

Bringing up a family of five on a busman's wage was not easy so poaching helped to put food on the table and pay the bills. My uncles from Hurlford were into it as well and were well known to the local polis. There was more than one night my dad never came home (as he'd spent the night in the cells), and another time they couldnae catch him but found his car where it had no right to be so removed the carburettor to curtail his nocturnal activities.

Some nights those activities involved rabbits, pheasants and deer. Other nights we'd slip into potato and turnip fields for an unscheduled midnight harvest, but dad's favourite was salmon fishing. He wisnae into all the fancy gear — just a net and a bottle of cyamax, which is like cyanide only far stronger. It didnae poison the fish, but it took all the oxygen out of the water and they'd all just float to the surface to be scooped up in nets by the McKinna brothers.

Being head of marketing and security meant it was my job to go first into the local pubs to make sure there were no polis about. If the coast was clear there'd be salmon and game for sale and the customers used to say they could taste the difference between a hook caught salmon and a cyamax salmon. The stress of fighting the hook made the flesh slightly bitter whereas the cyamax salmon was eased gently to sleep, with consequently sweeter flesh. Aye, poachers' customers were connoisseurs.

When not busy with poaching or watching Rangers, I was always playing football and soon developed the poacher's instinct for goals — sneaking in to score when I had no right to do so. Johnny on the Spot some call it, but it's not just luck — it's having the cunning to know where the ball is likely to wind up, the guile to get there before anyone else, and the technique to take advantage of any opportunity. Just like poaching.

I got plenty of goals through sheer pace (also an attribute of successful poachers) but most I scored from inside the six-yard box — either with my head, or by popping up where the opposition least wanted me to. Between the ages of 11 and 16 I honed my skills but I was never on the radar of any serious football club.

As for school, it had two excellent advantages. Besides being an acceptable football venue, school was also the place to meet girls.

Christine Kirkland was the year below me at Loudon Academy. She used to catch the school bus from Darvel and would occasionally see me crossing the paddock we used as a short cut. One day I was crossing the paddock with my mates, looking at some cows and wondering

My son Stuart was a striker like me – scoring goals is a thrill that never ever fades.

if one might fit into my dad's mini van, when they suddenly got the hump and charged us. We ran like hell and jumped through the fence at the side of the main road as all the double-decker buses were passing from Newmilns and Darvel. Christine happened to see our undignified flight from the stroppy beasts and found it tremendously amusing, but I didnae know she'd seen it until we started winching (which is Scottish for going out).

I met Christine through Shona Murphy who was Christine's friend. Shona was winching with my pal Jimmy Glover but they fell out, so she hooked up with me to make Jimmy jealous, and being a 15-year-old full of testosterone I was happy to oblige. Two weeks later, when I'd served my purpose, she broke up with me but softened the blow by saying her friend Christine liked me and that she would introduce

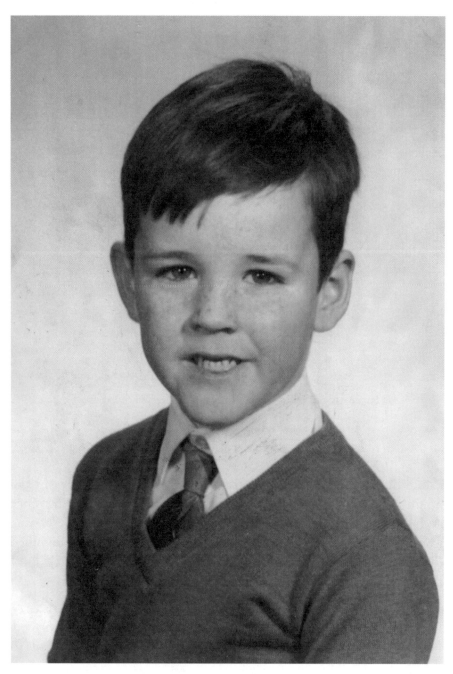

The poacher's son. Thieving salmon is a thrill that never ever fades.

us. So a day or two later my future wife and I met outside the home economics department and said a shy hello.

Christine just happened to mention that she was going to the youth club disco in Darvel Town Hall that Friday night. So, like a dog with a bone, I also just happened to be at the youth club disco and saw Christine with her pals, dancing around their handbags. I kept a low profile till the last dance which was a slow number, Chanson D'Amour by Manhattan Transfer, with that ra, da da, da da. I went up and tapped her on the shoulder and asked if she was dancing and she said aye, so we had a slow waltz around the Darvel Town Hall, and the dog had to be very careful not to let her know about the bone.

When the night finished I walked her to the top of the town just past the turning point for the bus. It had been snowing and everything was white under a full moon. We cuddled in the bus stop and then her mum and dad came by in their wee Bedford Van and shouted aggressively out the window: 'Are you right, pal?'

Aye, I was right, but I'd missed the last bus to Galston which was five miles so I had to walk all the way home at about midnight. But it was a great walk as I was so happy with myself to have had the balls to ask Christine to dance and even poached a kiss from her.

So we were officially winching. I was 15 years old and just three years later I'd be married and a father myself.

•   •   •

Lawrie finished school as soon as he reached 16 and started going around all the local factories, knocking on the back doors and asking for work. Work was still easy enough to get in those days so he found it quickly and life proceeded seamlessly from school to the lace factory. But the great constants of his life were still in place — football, Rangers and Christine.

The lace machine was a monster.

Over 20 metres long, weighed many, many tonnes and had thousands of moving parts, most of them heavy and razor sharp. Considering the delicacy of the lace produced it was a strangely brutal beast, and men all over the Valley were missing hands and fingers as a result of not paying it due attention and respect.

Just after my 16th birthday I started work at Stirling Bros in Darvel — lace manufacturers.

I started as a shuttler, filling shuttles with thread, and was then promoted to spooling, which meant putting new spools into the weaving machine as required. I was very young, fast and dextrous, and soon had a nice pair of silver-grey hands.

Aye, just like gorillas get a silver back when they come of age, lace weavers get silvery hands from handling the lead that greases the bars, and I was the youngest lacer in The Valley when they gave me my own machine. Cocky? Me? No fuckin' way!

One man who definitely wisnae cocky was Bobby Nesbitt. He was already retired when I started, but like so many gifted craftsmen he couldnae retire properly and worked a couple of days as a kind of unofficial supervisor who'd always seem to pop up just as he was needed. He wouldnae stand any carelessness or cheek and was always pulling me back into line — just as fast with either tongue or the back of his hand.

Bobby was a character straight out of the West Scotland traditional mould: mason, church beadle, working class intellectual, and supported Darvel Juniors, Kilmarnock and Rangers — in that order. Darvel Juniors were the local Valley semi-professional outfit, the equivalent of the Conference in England. Bobby was involved with the club so that might have been how I landed my job at Stirling Bros as I'd played a few games for Darvel at the end of the 76-77 season.

Most of my games had been off the bench so I was getting a bit jack of football. I'd accepted by that stage that I wisnae gaunny be a professional. But that didnae matter when I was 16 years old, and a silver-handed craftsman on £26 a week with a gorgeous girlfriend. I was already living the dream so I never bothered turning up for pre-season before the 77-78 season — much to Bobby's dismay. He was always at me saying, 'You're wasting your time Lawrie! You're too good not to be playing.'

'Aye,' I said, 'that's what I thought sitting on the bench last year.'

'You've got to pay your dues and bide your time,' he insisted, disgusted with my arrogance. 'You're only 16 in a team full of ex-professionals. You'll get your chance, but you've got to do it the coach's way.'

Well, I couldnae be told.

Another thing I couldnae be told about was the correct procedure when it came to fixing the spools. When these monstrous machines are running with the loom bar slashing back and forth, you have to watch the lace produced to check there's no problem. With so many moving parts it's easy for something to slip, so the lace starts coming out like it's been weaved by Pablo Picasso on magic mushrooms. Before too much cotton is wasted you've got to go through this difficult and irritating procedure to stop the machine, lock the bar in place, and then make your adjustments.

That's what the newbies do.

The seasoned pros, like me at 16, didnae bother with any of that namby pamby safety shite. Depending on the problem I just reached past the several tonnes of thrashing loom bar to nudge a spool back in place, or maybe paused the loom bar by locking the shuttle (but without stopping the machine). Bobby hated anyone to use the fast, easy route because it was fraught with danger — even locking the bar without stopping the machine was risky because tonnes of force were being held in rickety check and it could slip back into motion at any moment.

I trusted my reflexes though, and one day when I'd got the bar just paused — trembling with pent up violence while I reached down into the guts of the beast — I suddenly felt the machine lurch and knew I couldnae extract my hands in time. In the instant before tonnes of loom bar crushed my hands against the spools the machine suddenly died.

'What did I tell you?' shouted Bobby, who'd appeared like my guardian angel to hit the emergency kill lever. I'd never seen him so livid, but was extremely grateful to avoid serious permanent injury. I think I grew up a little that day and certainly I started taking Bobby's advice more seriously.

After my nasty fright with the lace machine my heart was no longer in it so I packed in that job. I spent all my severance pay (£120) on an engagement ring but Christine had to keep me for a couple of weeks while I waited to start another job, which I landed through my dad, driving a van for the local bakers — Brownings★ of Hurlford. I worked at Brownings for six months delivering rolls, cakes, pies and other baked goods between Hurlford and the gourmet centres of Mauchline, Auchinleck, Cumnock and New Cumnock.

I never lost touch with Bobby though and it was partly through his connections that I landed the plum job of van driver with Basford Dyers — collecting lace from the various factories, taking it to be dyed and then delivering it back to the factories. I worked with Christine's mum, Anne, in that place and also met Big Tam who worked in the delivery bay. Tam was a psychotically optimistic Kilmarnock fan, but more on him later.

After a year and a bit out of the game I started playing football again, mostly for Galston United but sometimes for the Catholic Youth Club, which did Bobby's head in. But they were easy to play for as they didnae bother training and I'd just show up for a run on a Saturday. It went deeply against his grain to be seen at a Catholic match (unless cheering for the opposition) but Bobby would occasionally turn up to watch, and at the end of the game he'd shake his head with disgust — especially if I'd scored, which wisnae too hard in that league — and say: 'You're wasting your time, Lawrie. You're too good for this. Get yasel back to Darvel Juniors.'

I suspect I was something like the son Bobby never had. He had a daughter but girls didnae play football in those days and they couldnae join the masons. When I joined up he gave me his father's apron that was 200 years old. (I've still got that apron — it's older than white settlement in Australia!) He was a powerful influence in my life — showed me the ropes and generally kept me on the straight and narrow.

But not that straight and narrow. One thing Bobby couldnae advise

★ Makers of the famous Killie Pie which won the award for best football ground pie in Britain two years running and was also the subject of a famous legal battle when the football club fell out with the bakers. Excellent pies though, and if you really are what you eat then I'd be about 42% Killie pie.

me about was Christine. We'd been winching since I was 15 and had grown so close you couldnae separate us with a crowbar, which led to her being pregnant at 18 with our first, Scott. I was 19, and we were hastily ushered into the church to tie the knot.

Bobby was there, watching over me with his usual blend of pride and shame. But more was to come. He'd saved my hands, and would soon be saving my football career.

3

'Hullo, Hullo,
We are the Billy Boys'

Glasgow Rangers Football Club was established in 1872 and was quickly the preferred club of the protestant half of the city.

It's difficult for someone not brought up in the Rangers tradition to fully appreciate what it means to the Billy Boys who follow their beloved Gers (or Teddy Bears). 'We are the people,' and 'We don't do walking away,' and 'Aye, Ready,' are some of their famous catch cries with layers of meaning impenetrable for the non-initiated.

Lawrie's brother in law, Jim Grimley (who was arrested by the Spanish police for invading the Nou Camp pitch in Barcelona after the UEFA Cup Winners Cup Final in 1972), tried to explain it: 'I'm not religious, but I dinnae like Catholics … not on match day.'

He said that in The Valley there was a fairly even divide between Celtic and Rangers fans and that when the Old Firm were playing the streets would be eerily deserted. Normally affable neighbours didn't want to encounter each other when passions were running high so kept warily indoors to watch or listen to the game that divided not just all of Scotland, but Scots all over the globe.

And the hate was strong. When Rangers fans entered Parkhead (Celtic's home ground) in those days they would all line up to piss on the walls (whether they needed to go or not!)

For those still living in Scotland and following Rangers, the word follow meant exactly that — to follow wherever they went. At the age of 17, Lawrie told Christine (almost his fiancée by now) that he was working the evening shift at the lace factory, which meant he wouldn't be able to see her for the next few nights. In reality, he was on his first ever Rangers road trip — to see his beloved Gers play Juventus in Turin. That was fraught with perils enough, but God help him if Christine found out.

The Runaway Lawrie

The barrel was at the front of the bus.

I was just turned 17 and on my first trip into Europe to see Rangers play Juventus in Turin, but that was the least of my concerns. I badly needed a piss and the bus was never gaunny stop just for me.

That meant the barrel.

There were fifty men on the bus — all of them sinking lagers since before we left Bridgeton Cross, but the bus wisnae stopping for toilet breaks so a steady stream of men kept up a steady stream into the barrel. We'd only stop when the barrel, our collective bladder, was full. And that wisnae gaunny happen in a hurry because some of the lads had rigged up a hose coming out of the barrel that they would use to spray passing motorists they didnae like the look of (i.e., most of them).

All I'd had was a couple of lemonades so I wisnae bothered, until somewhere south of Lincoln on the A1 I started to feel uncomfortable. I knew we'd have to stop at Dover to get on the ferry, but that was over two hours away and before we even reached the outskirts of London, I was faced with a serious dilemma.

I'd never been a drinker, which was unusual for a 17-year-old Scot. I didnae care much for the taste but it was the smell of stale beer when passing a pub that really turned me off. The whole bus stank of it and down towards the front, where the sloshing barrel lurked, was the worst.

In fact, I shouldnae have been there in the first place. Both my mother and Christine would've been furious if they knew, but I'd heard about the bus to Turin for the European Cup tie and despite none of my friends going, I somehow found myself aboard after telling Christine I was working afternoon shift for the week. She never saw me at such times so my sneaky tactic had reasonable prospects of success. But if I'd known about the barrel, I'd never have left the village.

Somewhere about Dartford, I knew it was either face the barrel or piss ma breeks — tough choice, but with an air of resignation I climbed to my feet and started walking down the aisle to join the queue.

Well, the smell was bad enough up the back of the bus. Towards the front it was diabolical: stale beer, unwashed bodies, garbage bags full of dead curry containers, and a barrel of rank piss. And to think I'd paid for the privilege!

Finally it was my turn and I can't begin to describe the sight that greeted me as I opened ma fly. Looking into that barrel was like looking into Satan's soul and a kind of steam seemed to rise off it like methane from a bog. I wisnae breathing that steam for all the tea in China so I held ma breath and tried to concentrate, but I wisnae used to playing in front of a crowd at that time. Stage fright! After holding on for hours I couldnae go and all the lads behind me were growling and jostling us to hurry up, so I had no choice but to breathe and it was like I could feel the evil entering my body and turning me into some toxic demon which is pretty much par for the course for any young Rangers fan on his first trip away.

Eventually I tinkled out ma two cans of lemonade and quickly made my escape back to the comparatively breathable stench at the back of the bus. And it must be said I felt different after pissing into the barrel; like I was accepted — one of the clan.

The felly I'd been sitting next to on the bus gave us a grin as I returned to my seat — if it's possible to grin with only six teeth. He bore all the hallmarks of the die-hard Rangers fan — tattoos, scars from knuckles and knives — but I felt somehow safe with him and wondered whether he might be able to protect me from Christine if she found out I wisnae at work.

Two hours later we stopped at Dover and there were a couple of hours to kill before the ferry to Calais, so naturally everyone went to the pub. There was nae bother getting into pubs underage back in those days, and even though I didnae drink I was really into the singing and camaraderie. But suddenly there's a raid! The polis are outside shouting with bullhorns, telling us to get out, and my mate with the tatts and the scars reaches down into his pants and pulls out a blade about 20 inches long.

'You look young and innocent,' he says, 'can you hold ma chib for us?'

I was too terrified to even move so he snarls with disgust and hides his blade in an aspidistra and we troop outside to where the polis are all in riot gear and telling us to line up. It seems some of the lads had been emptying the barrel and had seen fit to splash it over some tourists who'd strayed too close, and possibly spoken in Italian, which was ill-advisable when Rangers are playing Juventus.

The polis have got these piss-drenched Johnny Foreigners to show them who was responsible, and they're pointing out everyone! So the polis tell them to get lost and just decide for themselves who must've been guilty, including my mate with tatts and scars.

'We'll let youse go after the ferry's gone,' the polis say to these blokes, all of whom were probably innocent (at least of the barrel splashing). As my mate's being led away he gives me a look and a nod back towards the pub, obviously meaning to go and fetch his chib, but there was no way I was gaunny be caught with what could well have been a murder weapon in its time, so I gave him a look of baffled incompetence so I couldnae be blamed later.

'Ma fuckin' chib ya doss prick!' he shouts, but fortunately the polis didnae understand his accent.

•   •   •

13 September 1978

We got to Turin, after crossing the Alps, about 36 hours after boarding the ferry. It was Wednesday morning in early autumn, crisp and clear — but the city didnae know what was in store.

About a thousand Rangers fans had made the journey in buses, trains and cars. The whole working week dedicated to one game of football on the Wednesday night. But not just any game. This was the first leg of a European Champions Cup tie, against one of the best teams in Europe.

We were in a frightful state after 48 hours on the road — sleeping in our seats, or on the floor, which was awash with lager and piss. We absolutely stank, and it was no wonder the locals gave us such a wide berth as we staggered about the town wrapped in our sodden Union

Jacks and shouting: 'Il Papa di Morto,' which someone had told us meant 'Death to the Pope!'

Old habits …

But for all that, relations with the Juventus fans were surprisingly cordial. We even managed to strike up a game with them in the afternoon. It was about a 100 men a side in this huge park in the middle of town, with hundreds more crowded around the edges, kicking any poor bastard who came close enough, from either side. I think we won that by about 50 broken teeth to 37.

Then it was time for the game. It was a profoundly moving experience to be standing among the thousand Rangers fans, out-singing 69,000 Italians (with the aid of a thousand airhorns we'd brought along to drown out the Juve fans whenever they got a head of steam up). The Rangers team was full of the heroes who'd won the treble* the previous season under Jock Wallace — Peter McCloy in goals, Sandy Jardine, Colin Jackson, Alex McDonald, Tommy McLean. And up front of course, the brilliant Bobby Russell, Derek Johnstone and my personal hero Gordon Smith.

The game itself was a scrappy affair won by the Italians by the only goal, and we all trooped out of the stadium more than chuffed with our efforts. One nil down was a good result and we were more than confident, as we made our way singing back to the buses, that we'd easily turn the tables back at Ibrox for the second leg.

We sang too soon.

Suddenly, out of the darkness came swarming hundreds of Red Brigade terrorists who'd been marching for some stupid cause, but then they'd heard about the match and forgot their shite commie politics to come and sort out the Rangers lads.

Absolute fucking bedlam. My mate with the tatts and scars had somehow found his way to the match after missing the ferry and ran screaming at me, 'Where's ma chib?'

'It's on the bus … I think,' I said.

---

* The treble: the Scottish League Cup, the Scottish Premier League trophy and the Scottish FA Challenge Cup.

He didnae need his chib. The man was a maniac and by sticking close I got back to the bus relatively unharmed. But the bus was surrounded, and then the bricks and bottles started flying. The front window vanished in a shower of glass as a cinder block was heaved through and then the bus was rocking as hundreds of crazed Red Brigadiers attacked from either side, trying to turn us over.

The driver managed to start the engine and we cleared a path through the rubble and bodies with just four windows unsmashed as the sirens started wailing in the distance and the Red Brigade vanished as quickly as they'd appeared.

'Where's ma fuckin' chib?' the lad with the tatts and scars asked me once again.

I finally came clean. 'Sorry mate … I lost it, in all the fuss just now.'

'Good lad,' he said, with a wink and grin, and I realised he thought I'd lost it in the fight — maybe by inserting it into some Italian's guts. I saw no reason to set him straight. The less said about the missing chib the better.

• • •

That night and the next day were absolute torment — driving across the Alps in autumn, in a bus with no windows, all of us wrapped in our Union Jacks as a futile extra layer of non-existent warmth. It was 20 below zero with the wind chill factor and our hands and faces were as blue as our Rangers hearts.

The highlight of the journey home was when we stopped at the Eiffel Tower. A thousand Rangers fans — pissed, stinking and filthy stormed up the tower waving flags and singing. This was the time that punk rock was at its peak and with all our Union Jacks and Rangers flags draped over the top of the tower we must have looked like some kind of surreal backdrop to a Sex Pistols movie: Anarchy for the Champs Elysees!

But for all the fun, my conscience was starting to play havoc with me about what I was gaunny say to Christine. She had a vicious temper and a way of knowing instantly if I was being less than direct with her, so I started thinking up methods of appeasement, which has always been the British way when confronted with a warmongering dictator.

I only had a little money left after four days on the road, and despite it meaning I'd not be able to eat or drink for the last day, I spent the last of my cash on the most romantic present I could afford — a carton of Rothmans.

Finally I made it back to Galston on Friday night — tired, hungry and filthy. I couldnae even speak with all the shouting and singing, so it didnae take long for Christine to deduce that my sorry and disgusting condition was not the result of four nights evening shift in the lace factory.

'Ye went to Turin?' she cried, in exasperated fury. 'Without me?'

'I got ye a present,' I defended, and pulled out the carton of Rothmans.

'Fags? You go to Italy spending money for our honeymoon, and all I get is some fags?'

She told me where I could stick the present. I suppose if she'd unwrapped them and done it one at a time, it might just have been possible.

4

'Do you want to be a professional footballer, son?'

Around the ages of 18/19 young Lawrie had quite a lot on his plate. He had steady work as a van driver at Basford Dyers, he was newly married to Christine, having his first son and all his spare time was taken up following Rangers about. He had no time for football and spent a season or two out of the game, but it called him back.

When I started playing again, they called me Shergar — after the nippy sprinter that won the Epsom by ten lengths in 1981. I didnae have incredible skill but I was tall, strong, good with my head and very fast. I was playing for Galston United in the local kick-about league and sheer weight of goals, plus the intervention of Bobby Neil, saw me invited to play for Darvel Juniors who were the number one team in The Valley. This was the first time I was actually paid to play football with hard cash rather than black market pontoon cards to sell in the doorways of pubs. I was paid the princely sum of five pounds per week, but that's more than it sounds. You could have a good night out in those days for £5 — a few drinks and a fish supper with my pliant wife. I was living the dream.

Some of my mates used to come and watch Darvel Juniors play and every time I got into the clear the stands would ring with cries of 'Go Shergar!' I was surprised to discover myself a fairly strong player at that level and found the job of scoring goals not too difficult. I was newly married, newly bairned, enjoying my football and getting £5 a week for it. Life couldnae get any better.

Aye, it could. My life changed the day the scout from Greenock

Morton came to watch Darvel Juniors. He was the archetypal stranger on the sidelines wearing a raincoat and cloth cap — the traditional uniform of football scouts and flashers. He spoke to me after one of my first games and asked was I interested in signing professional papers. Of course I was, but this was a bit of a shock. Despite the fact I'd been telling my mother since I was five that I was gaunny play for Rangers and buy her a Hillman Avenger, and despite the fact I'd been preparing all my life by keeping a ball glued to my foot wherever I went — the idea of professional football was not something I'd seriously contemplated after the age of 10. I'd never even made one of the junior representative teams, and yet here was a complete stranger telling me I was good enough for Greenock Morton in the third tier of the Scottish league!

I know what you're thinking because I was thinking it too — he's no scout, he's a flasher. But once the thought got into my head that maybe I was good enough for professional football, I couldnae get it out. From that moment I was focused on football like never before. I trained hard and on match days I'd be a bundle of nerves, wondering whether the scout would be back, with a contract maybe. And as a consequence, my game completely fell apart.

'Shergar?' sneered the coach after yet another ineffectual performance. 'You're more like Trigger you dopey fuckin' plodder!'

In the next four games I only got the one goal and played so shite I was not remotely surprised that the scout hadnae reappeared. I'd dared to dream and my footballing shortcomings had been immediately exposed to put me back in the box where I belonged. Or so I thought.

Every Sunday morning, in those days, we'd go round to Christine's mum's for a fry up. I was sitting there reading the papers and tucking into the traditional bacon, eggs, beans on toast, black pudding and passive cigarette smoke when a car pulled up in the driveway. Three club members got out — Billy Duncan, Bobby Graham and Sandy Peckham. I was a bit concerned as I watched their approach through the window. They looked like a mob of villains off *The Sweeney* so I was worried I'd pissed them off somehow.

But instead of storming the house with a sawn off shooter and stockings over their heads, they knocked politely and had very good news indeed. It turns out that Sandy Peckham (who ran a double glazing company) had been dealing with Jim McLean from Dundee United. In the course of their negotiations, Jim (an ex-Kilmarnock player) asks whether Darvel Juniors have got any decent prospects. 'There's a young striker,' says Sandy. Before I know it, I'm being offered a trial with Dundee United.

So a couple of days later my dad (who'd never seen me play since I was a wee lad) drives me, Billy Duncan and Bobby Nesbitt from the lace factory up to Dundee, and from there we follow the team bus up to Brechin. The game was Dundee Reserves versus Brechin firsts on a ground that sloped so much you had to abseil into the penalty box. I got the only goal of the game with a left footed volley from 20 metres but afterwards Jim McLean said to me: 'You're good enough for senior football … but not here. You're too old.'

I was only twenty for heaven's sake! But my dream wisnae quite dashed. Jim rang Kilmarnock (my local professional club) and so I waited for our phone to ring.

The day after the Scottish Cup Final in '78. I was thinking about a certain policeman.

Christine with our firstborn, Scott.

When it did, it was Ayr United (Scottish second division) that wanted me for a trial, but I had a strained groin and couldnae make it. Then the phone rang again, and this time it was Kilmarnock asking if I could come in for a trial against St Mirren Reserves at Rugby Park — home ground of the mighty Killie where I'd been many times as a spectator but never as a player. We lost 4-2 but I got both goals and they asked me to play against Motherwell Reserves the following week. About the same time, Motherwell contacted Darvel Juniors wanting me to play in the same game — against Killie!

It's no wonder the giants of the lower leagues were all chasing me because my performance in that match was one of my best ever. Scouts (or flashers) from several clubs were in attendance, plus Big Jim Clunie, coach of Kilmarnock. I wisnae too nervous that night and everything I touched turned to goals. When the final whistle blew I was striding off the park, ten foot tall, with four in the bag. I could see the Motherwell officials waiting to talk to me on the sideline but Davie Wilson, assistant coach of Kilmarnock collars me and says: 'Stay away from those vultures! You're coming with me.'

He takes me straight through the tunnel, up the stairs and into the boardroom, still in my muddy, wet gear, and there's Big Jim — as close to smiling as I ever saw him — with a pen and paper.

'Do you want to be a professional footballer, son?'

I didnae even ask the terms, I was that excited. I just signed, and was pleasantly surprised to learn that I was getting £1000 sign-on fee, £10 a week in the off season, £50 a week during the season, plus £10 a point. If we won it meant £70, which almost doubled my wages from the dyers. Almost no-one was a full-time professional in those days, in Scotland at least. Most players still had at least a part-time job, especially in the off season, but out of nowhere I'm seeing more money than I'd ever dreamt of. That Hillman Avenger was suddenly a realistic proposition.

It was strange going back to work after that. The Valley was buzzing with the news and everywhere I went in my van they were lining up to shake my hand or slap me on the back. But professional football wisnae all heroes and hat tricks.

My first game as a Kilmarnock professional was the following weekend playing in the Reserves.

Against Rangers.

At Ibrox.

.   .   .

The Catholics have got St Peters Basilica; the Moslems have got Mecca; salmon have got the pond in which they were spawned — we've all got some place we revere as our Holy of Holies. For me it was Ibrox. I'd been many times since I was eleven to watch the mighty Gers and sing with the Billy Boys, but to turn up there in the Killie team bus to actually grace the hallowed turf as a player — even if it was only Reserves — was still the achievement of my personal Mecca.

We entered through the famous blue gates and were immediately in a part of the stadium I'd never seen before. The part that's off-limits to the public — sacred ground to be graced only by the footballing nobility. And me.

Taking the players' entrance at Ibrox was a profoundly moving moment. The walls are oozing history, covered with pictures of old teams, players and managers. I felt a sense of awe and unworthiness to be even looking at those pictures and half expected some steward to grab me by the collar, give me an earful about knowing my place and turf me out.

But there I was, sitting in the Ibrox dressing room — stunned to think of the players who'd come through the same room to take on the mighty Gers and I felt a very odd blend of pride and guilt as I donned the blue and white Kilmarnock strip. I was proud to be a professional, but what sort of treacherous viper plays against the team he's always supported so passionately?

We left the dressing room and my heart was beating like a jack-hammer. I could see the turf at the end of the tunnel like a square patch of green heaven and I'm no longer aware of my feet. It's like I'm floating — having some out-of-body experience as the green square gets larger and then bursts into light as I'm outside, staring up at the (almost) empty stands where I'd stood shoulder to shoulder with the passionate horde singing about 1690 and the Battle of the Boyne, just wanting to kill any bastard that wisnae wearing blue.

I'm running out ontae the pitch and inside my head I'm singing:

Hullo, Hullo,
We are the Billy Boys,
Hullo, Hullo,
You'll know us by our noise,
We're up to our knees in Fenian blood,
Surrender or you'll die,
For we are the Bridgeton Derry Boys.

This is *the* Rangers song — the most hallowed and frowned upon song in these depressingly PC days. I'd been singing it out loud just the previous weekend in the Copeland Road End amid the Blue Sea of Ibrox as Rangers contested the title with Alex Ferguson's Aberdeen. We didnae really mean any harm (and it's just a lullaby these days), but there I was, fighting for the enemy in my home camp, and feeling like the Pope would feel caught blowing his nose on the Shroud of Turin.

We got flogged 6-0.

I had a totally shite game, which is hardly surprising when I got no service. But why would a team pass the ball to their new striker who's applauding and cheering everything the opposition do? I was totally star-struck, as I've never been before or since, and it was absolutely the worst game I ever played.

But at least I was able to contribute to a Rangers victory.

• • •

Lawrie played 87 games for Kilmarnock in the Scottish Premier League and 1st Division between 1982 and 1986 scoring 17 goals. His first team debut was at Rugby Park against Hibernian in August 1982.

I'd signed on the Tuesday night for Kilmarnock near the end of the season, played that game against Rangers Reserves, but I'd been given permission to play Darvel's last game against Beith Juniors (an arrangement that wouldnae be allowed in these unsentimental, by-the-book FIFA days). It was the usual vicious affair between Darvel and Beith but at the end I shook hands with Stevie Clark★, the Beith centre half, who like me was about to turn professional with St Mirren. It was an exciting time. Like the Australian NPL or the English Conference today, the Juniors was a league full of old ex-pros and young up-and-comers and I remember the sense of achievement I felt talking to Stevie, knowing we'd both graduated into the big league.

Kilmarnock were near the top of the 1st Division, which was the step below the Scottish Premier League. But we were almost certain to be promoted with one game to play, so the following weekend I'm sitting in the posh seats behind the bench in a suit and Kilmarnock tie, watching the first team smash Queen of the South six doughnut. This was it! In just a few months I'd gone from kick-about park football to SPL!

Well, that was easier said than done.

• • •

Turning up for pre-season training for the first time as a professional player was like I'd been abducted by aliens and taken to a different planet — just breathing the air tastes different when you do it as a pro footballer. I was 20 years old and a bit shy, but chuffed to bits to find my training gear all set out in my own special corner of the dressing room at Rugby Park. I already knew Ian Bryson, who was a friend of Christine's from school, and Jimmy Clarke, one of the senior players, who was a friend of Christine's dad. But apart from that they were all just faces off the telly or the back pages of the *Daily Record*.

One I got to know quickly was Coby (Jimmy Cockburn) who was the team comedian.

'Who the fuck is this?' demanded Coby, confronting me with his arm round a drooling maniac, who was totally naked with his cock tied in a bow.★★ 'If you're gaunny join the team you've got to pass the initiation.'

★ Stevie Clark was brother of Kilmarnock captain Robert, he went on to play for Chelsea.
★★ The drooling maniac remains a close friend so I'd prefer not to reveal his identity.

Thankfully I was laughing too much to ever find out what the initiation was, or maybe that's how you passed — by laughing instead of running screaming from the room?

They took us out to Dean Park which had this natural amphitheatre and got us to start running up and down the hill. Naturally, as the new young buck, I couldnae help showing off by bolting early, despite the warnings of the older boys, and before I knew it I'm down on the ground heaving up my breakfast.

'Telt ya, ya stupid cunt,' laughed Coby, trotting past breezily. But I didnae care. I was absolutely in my element on my first morning of professional pre-season. Even throwing my guts up was fun because that's what professionals do in pre-season (and by the end of the morning pretty much everyone had emptied the carrot sack). I may have had sick all down the front of my shirt but I'd never been so proud.

There were 30-odd players in the squad — first team and reserves — so I knew it widnae be easy breaking into the first team. Pretty much the whole pre-season I played in the Reserves, with an occasional foray off the bench for the first team in games that didnae matter. Through sheer hard work and physical presence I gradually won the confidence of the other players and, as the season proper approached, I like to think I was putting pressure on the first team strikers with strong performances (and quite a few goals) in the Reserves.

Mind you, I didnae expect to make the first team, so was totally gobsmacked on the Thursday night before the first league match to see L McKinna on the teamsheet to play Hibs at home. I couldnae believe my eyes! I'd made a couple of cameos off the bench but didnae seriously think I was in Jim Clunie's plans for the first team — not straight away.

I went back to check the sheet, just to make sure my eyes werenae playing tricks. And sure enough, L McKinna was still there, but so were quite a lot of other names. That's odd, I thought, but didnae worry too much about it. I couldnae wait to get home and tell Christine and her parents, but I also drove my Basford Dyers van round to Bobby Nesbitt's to give him the news. He couldnae have been more proud and his eyes misted over a little — I think mine might have as well — and he shook my hand (which I was lucky still to have after that incident with the lace machine).

'Always knew you could do it Lawrie,' he said, and I realised how much I owed him. Without Bobby's intervention I might not even be playing, let alone playing professional.

Christine and her dad, Rab, were beside themselves with excitement but I was still wondering why there were so many names on the list. Maybe it was an extended list to be cut before the match? My own excitement started to cool as I realised I was one of the more likely to be cut, and I started subtly trying to dampen the expectations of my family.

But The Valley was buzzing. The following day, everywhere I went in my van, there were people crowding round to shake my hand and give me advice about Hibs. 'I'm sure I won't be starting,' I kept saying. 'Dinnae be so fuckin' modest,' was the typical response. 'Lawrie's gaunny tear the Hibbees a new arse!' reckoned Big Tam, holding court in the delivery bay at Basford Dyers. It was all getting a bit out of control because the more I thought about it, the more I realised 20 names didnae go into 11 places.

On the Saturday, I dressed in my club suit and tie and made my way down to Rugby Park. Rab dropped me at the big front door and as I got out with my gear bag there's a bit of a cheer and all these people crowd about wanting my autograph. It was surreal. It'd never occurred to me that people might want my scribbled name on bits of paper, but that's part of being a professional so I got stuck in.

Big Tam was there waiting for me. 'Are you playing Big Man?'

'I'll let you know as soon as I find out myself,' I told him and ventured through the front door, for the first time in my gear and hoping to play. I'd been there a million times before by this point but the corridors of football power seemed different on match day — like all the ghosts of players past are lining the walls and watching — breathing a sense of history and destiny into your lungs as you stride towards the home team dressing room.

The room was full of excitement (like any team at any level) before the first game of the season, but there was something else — a strange undercurrent that somehow added an edge to the team's collective angst. I was looking around, wondering where some of the senior players were and that's when I found out …

'They're on strike,' muttered Ian Bryson. 'Werenae too chuffed about the board lowering the bonus money from £20 to £10 a point.'

I was still trying to absorb this when Davie Wilson, the assistant coach, puts his arm round my shoulder. 'How you feeling Big Man?

'Not so bad, Davie.'

'That's good, because you're on the bench.'

I'd pretty much talked myself into believing that I widnae be playing so the bench was a huge bonus, even if it was only happening because of a players' strike. I ran back out to tell Tam, even though the team line-up was supposed to be secret.

'What do you know about this fuckin' players' strike?' asked Tam. He knew more about the team politics than I did!

Back in the room the atmos was now a little subdued, but I was on a personal high. Pulling on the blue and white Kilmarnock strip for the first time before an SPL match was one of those special life moments where you're trying to concentrate on the experience and extract every last drop of it to file in your memory — like parachuting for the first time, or losing your virginity.

I don't remember a single word of Jim Clunie's pre-match message. Hibs were a strong team in those days and all I could think about was that it was only a couple of years since I used to wait with some of the other Rangers hoodlums on the edge of town after Hibs matches.* The Hibs bus had to take the road out of Kilmarnock back to Edinburgh that wound through a small village with tight streets and by the church the bus had to slow right down. We werenae bothered with the team bus, it was the supporters buses we wanted. When they almost stopped

---

* Hibs, being a Catholic club, were the Edinburgh version of Celtic so Killie v Hibs matches would attract plenty of Old Firm supporters wanting someone to hate when their own teams werenae playing.

by the church we'd jump out from behind the wall and pelt them with rocks (we couldnae afford eggs). The Hibbee casuals would all jump out to chase us but they'd always been drinking lager and couldnae go uphill as fast as the clean living Killie boys.

This is all going through my head as Jim says, 'Right … you got that Lawrie?'

'Aye, boss.'

We went out for a warm up and all I can hear is Tam and a few of the old Loudon Academy boys, already shouting to give Lawrie McKinna a go — a chant they kept up throughout the first half. And shortly after half time there was a huge cheer when Jim Clunie told me to go and warm up.

Jogging past my mates and family to go and warm up was a truly weird but uplifting sensation. I didnae really have a proper warm up routine so I must have looked a bit of a clown — trotting about behind the goals, stretching, feeling terribly self-conscious.

The strike-weakened team had put up a decent fight, but we'd been 1-0 down at halftime, and then midway through the second half it's two.

'Lawrie!'

I looked up at Jim Clunie who's beckoning as the Hibs players celebrate in front of their own bench just a few metres away.

'Get on and have a go, Big Man!'

When I stood up and walked to the halfway, the roar from the stand behind me was like a blast of joyful thunder. The love in the air was thick enough to carve and I felt like I was walking on a trampoline as I entered the pitch. The players all looked like giants but I got an early touch, shielded the ball away from John Brownley (a Scottish national team player) and played the ball in behind him for Ian Bryson to chase. It came to nothing but straight away I knew I could do it. I had the strength and technique to play at that level. And I truly knew I had the measure of Brownley when he tried to break my leg about a minute later!

Christine knows she's got a good catch — she's the only one smiling!

Kilmarnock FC 1982. How on earth did I go from kickabout league
to playing with this lot?

I got a few shots away and a couple of headers but didnae trouble the scoreboard attendant. And in a flash it was over. Twenty minutes had passed in a rosy blur and our depleted side had put in a creditable performance, going down only 2-0 to one of the best teams in Scotland. I was walking about in a daze, shaking hands with household names in Hibs shirts. 'Well played,' said John Brownley, an international defender who knew he'd been in a match with Lawrie McKinna. In that moment I knew I belonged in the SPL.

The following week I was back in Reserves.

• • •

The players' strike only lasted a week so the tried and trusted strike pairing of Gallagher and Bryson were once again leading the line for Kilmarnock while Lawrie McKinna went back to the stiffs to learn his trade.

I learned it well. SPL was a hard gig but I was a strong player in Reserves and kept the statisticians busy calculating my goals to games ratio. The six-yard box was Lawrie Land where I was always pouncing on loose balls and scoring plenty with my head — especially the far post run where I could really get up and hang for crosses and corners. An aggressive centre forward who can get his head as high as the keeper's hands — that's a valuable player to have. So a couple of months later I was back on the bench for the first team — at home again, against Celtic.

This time when I got on the pitch I reverted to type. I'd spent so much of my youth hurling abuse at Celtic from the stands of Rugby Park, Ibrox and Parkhead that I simply couldnae help myself. Roy Aitken may have been the Scotland captain, but he was also the Celtic captain so I smashed him — I might never have had another opportunity — and was rewarded with my first SPL yellow card.

Later, back at home, mum was furious with me because the commentators on Radio Westsound had been scathing about young Lawrie McKinna who seemed to have no interest in the game other than kicking fuck out of the Celtic players. But you can hardly blame me. Kick some green-hooped bastard on the street and you might get gaol. Do it on the park and all you get is a card! It's a brilliant system.

Mind you, I got smashed myself in my next match which was the first leg of a League Cup tie against Dundee United. I went up for a header with Richard Gough and managed to put him on his arse. I'd hit him pretty hard but he never said a word — just dusted himself off and got on with it — but there was something almost eerie about his grim silence and I felt a wee chill as it occurred to me the large and famously violent Scottish international might be plotting revenge.

A few minutes later, the ball's bounced high over near the sideline and I'm in that particularly vulnerable position of having to wait for it to come down so I can get up and nod it on. I'm looking only at the ball when I suddenly thought: 'Where the fuck is Gough?'

He couldnae have timed it more perfectly. Just as I jumped, a force like a derailed freight train slammed into my side and I thumped onto my back on the cinder track that surrounded Tannadice. Somehow I struggled through to the end of the game but I was in a bad way and subsequent X-rays showed two cracked ribs.

A week later I ran into Goughy in the tunnel before the return leg. 'Good luck tonight,' he says, and I had to say, 'I'm not playing. You broke my ribs last week.' To his credit he was quite upset and apologetic — even managed to scrounge a bunch of unused complimentary tickets from his team mates for my friends and family.

Ribs were a bit of a recurring problem for me. I may have cracked them at Dundee but I broke them at Lesser Hampden against Queens Park Reserves. I'm through one-on-one with the keeper and slid in just ahead of him to get my toe to the ball, but he's also slid and his knees hit me in the chest so I'm lying on the ground, gasping in agony, watching the ball trickle over the line for a goal.

I wisnae celebrating. It's interesting the way injured players are treated these days compared with back then — no motorised carts with paramedics back in the early 80s. And no heated change rooms with all the modern first aid equipment. They just left me in the back of the dark and freezing dressing room, curled in a ball of misery, until my dad turned up at 11pm to collect me in his Western SMT bus.

If I got no sympathy from paramedics, the family were worse.

'Don't give us yer shite! It's only broken fuckin' ribs,' says Christine's dad, Rab, in disgust as Christine and her mum fussed about making me comfortable. But it's funny how life can be so quickly ironic sometimes. Only a week or so later, poor Rab's in a car accident and cops a broken sternum. Aye … several broken ribs. I felt for the poor bastard, but I could see the funny side. He couldnae.

Aye, tough gig the SPL. Kilmarnock were relegated at the end of that season with me just making a handful of appearances off the bench. The following year we were in Division One and I found myself a regular starter.

5

The Magic of the Cup

Some of Lawrie's finest moments on the pitch came against Sir Alex Ferguson's all-conquering Aberdeen — part of the New Firm of the middle 80s. The 3rd Round of the Scottish FA Cup in 1983/84 saw the Scottish Champions drawn against lowly Kilmarnock where a tall young striker was just starting to get established.

Big Tam was my biggest fan.

Some people said he was not quite right in the head, but I'll never agree with that. The boy had sound judgment.

Tam was Killie to the core and always wore his kit — to work, to bed, under his suit on his wedding day. He bled blue blood, worked at Basford Dyers in the delivery bay, and watched every game that Kilmarnock played. That meant he saw plenty of Lawrie McKinna and always had an opinion as to how I'd played the morning after.

'Did well last night, Big Man,' he'd say as I backed my van up to his service bay if I'd scored. 'No so well,' he'd lament, keeping me waiting for my load after a loss or when he disapproved of my form.

It was Tam that first told me we were drawn against the champions. A bolt of pure fear hit me in the chest, mingled with awe, and the two emotions chased each other round my head for the next few days. I could barely walk, let alone concentrate on training or work.

In those days I was on the edge of the first team, mostly coming off the bench, but I knew there'd be a fair chance I'd play. Against Aberdeen — Scottish champions with half the national team in their ranks! How was it possible that a part-time van driver from Darvel was about to lace up a boot against the likes of Jim Leighton, Alex McLeish, Doug Rougvie and Gordon Strachan? And managed by the new wunderkind of Scottish football — Alex Ferguson — who had turned a team of nobodies from the arse-end of nowhere into Scottish and European Champions.

No-one thought we could possibly win the game, except Tam. At every opportunity he'd be in my ear telling me his theories about how to beat Leighton or get past Rougvie. No-one else was bothered. Even the players were just seeing the game as a chance to go autograph hunting!

Well, we had to wait for that. Scotland in February is always cold and black, but that year it was like even hell had frozen over. Daylight lasted about four hours and there was never water in the tap because the pipes were frozen. The houses were locked in with snow and the idea of 'warmth' was just a crazy concept from a sci-fi movie. When we weren't at work we sat huddled around the fire or the radiator covered with blankets while the house was buried in ever-deeper layers of white.

Going to work was bad enough. Getting in and out of a draughty van all day with every road in the Valley covered in black ice was extremely unpleasant. But after work was when the real torment began — going to training.

Sometimes we'd just be inside the club rooms running on the spot and doing push-ups with the pitch under a yard of snow. But other times they'd have ploughed the snow away and we'd turn up to train on frozen mud. No matter what you wore it'd be wet within seconds, and no matter how hard you worked you could never get warm with an Arctic wind off the Irish Sea blowing your wet gear against your body and making you feel that if you stopped for more than a second you'd be snap-frozen into a statue in honour of misery.

Three times the game against Aberdeen was postponed because the weather was not just bad, it was impossible. It was a four-hour bus drive from Kilmarnock to Pittodrie Park but, with all the snow, the roads were as impenetrable as the famous Aberdeen back four. We couldnae get through.

After yet a fourth postponement, they decided the game simply had to go ahead — rain, hail or blizzard. So on Monday the 13th of February I finished work early, went home for a shower (the pipes were only unfrozen around the middle of the day), caught the district bus down to Kilmarnock, walked to Rugby Park to catch the team bus, and we were off to the East Coast. (I'd like to see Cristiano Ronaldo having to walk and get two buses to a game!)

For all the difficult conditions, it was pure excitement on the bus. 'I'm gauny break Strachan's fuckin' leg,' Coby kept telling us. 'That's if I can catch the bastard.'

Jim Clunie was clearly not averse to such tactics. He never told Coby to mind his tongue, and whenever I came off the bench, his last words of instruction were always: 'First corner … put the keeper on his arse!'

We stopped, as usual, at Stonehaven for our traditional pre-game snack. It was a scientific diet of scrambled eggs, beans on toast and roast chicken specially designed to fuel professional athletes through 90 minutes of football in Scottish conditions.

About 6.00 pm we reached Pittodrie and it was already blacker than Satan's skivvy and cold as the chancellor's heart. The snow had been scraped off the pitch and we went out to warm up in front of 15,000 Aberdeen fans who were already having a party. We were not to be taken seriously as opposition — we were just the cannon fodder needed to help usher their heroes through to the fourth round!

Then came the bad news: I wisnae starting. That meant sitting on the bench enduring the Arctic wind, but without being able to run about to try and stay unfrozen. Still, I was distracted from the cold by the quality of the footballers we were up against — household names the lot of them, driven on by the sheer force of Alex Ferguson's will. He was already a very animated character on the bench and demanded excellence at 100 decibels using highly colourful language. A seriously passionate man.

From the very start we were just hanging on. Eric Black hit the bar with a header, then right on half time had a goal ruled out for offside. We lost Derek McDicken with a nasty head injury and midway through the second half, my mate Ian Bryson just about had his head taken off (accidentally I'm sure) by Doug Rougvie. Ian's nose was badly broken and he couldnae continue.

'Can you do a job, Big Man?'

I looked up and there was Jim Clunie, staring down at me.

'Aye,' I said, eager for the chance to run and get my blood circulating.

'Right … now, first corner …'

'Ye want us to sit Leighton on his arse?'

'Good lad.'

He patted me on the shoulder and I stripped off the tracksuit, immediately feeling the cold like blades of ice cutting into my numbed flesh.

I came on with 25 minutes left, and the difference in standard was fantastic. Aberdeen were simply effortless the way they kept the ball, but somehow we got a corner, and with Big Jim's instructions front of mind I ran straight at Leighton as the ball was swung over. But I might as well have run at the Wallace Monument. The words 'brick' and 'shithouse' come to mind, and it was L McKinna who wound up on his arse after bouncing off the Scottish international keeper like a squash ball.

Leighton was bad enough but the worst part of my job was to be marked by Doug Rougvie who played centre half. The man was barely human — huge, hairy and growling — and it was like being marked by a grizzly bear. An exceptionally fast and intelligent grizzly, because every time the ball came near he'd nip in ahead but still find time to kick shite out of me or give me a wallop with his massive paw.

With full time in sight we finally went a goal down when Peter Weir scored and the fight seemed to go out of us. It was like we'd agreed a truce. It was too cold to do much more than huddle together like penguins, so we stayed at our end and Aberdeen stayed their end, and the 15,000 in the stands just shivered and willed the pace of time to speed up so they could get home to their fires with their one goal win.

The turning point came at the end of normal time. Alan McCulloch punted the ball out and (as usual) it was coming down straight onto Rougvie's head, but in a moment of desperate inspiration I leapt like a salmon (the type that Rougvie would normally catch in his claws at waterfalls), somehow got to the ball first and nodded it past him shouting 'Gally!'

Brian Gallagher needed no further invitation. He was off in a flash, one on one with Leighton, and smashed the ball into the top corner.

Silence.

Silence, except for the referee's whistle and the outraged fury of Alex Ferguson.

There wisnae any of the hugging and kissing you see these days when players celebrate a goal. It was more of a manly handshake, or maybe a pat on the shoulder with your more intimate team mates. We ran back to halfway after a reserved and dour celebration in the Presbyterian masonic tradition, grimly expressing our determination to stay in the game.

As for myself, I was delighted to have made a contribution with almost my first touch. Rougvie was less impressed. He took his vengeance at every opportunity, probably already aware of the bollocking he would get from Ferguson if they didnae snatch the win.

Extra time was excruciating, and seemed to go forever. Aberdeen were camped in our third, pressing around our goal with McCulloch playing out of his skin — palming shots onto the crossbar, diving at Strachan's feet to snatch the ball off his laces. There was one agonising moment when the ball fell to Strachan about six yards out with an open goal. He had to score but he's tried to hit it too hard and the groan from the crowd as the ball flashed over the bar was pure music to Kilmarnock ears.

Seconds later, the final whistle blew and I was exultant with joy and sheer relief.

After kicking lumps out of me for 20 minutes, Doug Rougvie shook my hand and said: 'Aye, well played.' In its own way, it was one of the best compliments I ever had as a player, but the lads were pleased with my efforts, also. As was the boss, despite my failure to follow instructions

Above: Big Tam's wedding day. He had his Killie strip under his suit but spent his wedding night cowering under the bed.

Scott and Stuart preparing for their Killie debuts.

and put Leighton in the back of the net. 'Well done, Lawrie,' he said, but I was barely listening as the cold settled deep in my bones. I was so cold I couldnae even shiver, but fortunately inside the change room there was one of those huge communal baths. We just fell into it — the room full of steam and warmth and excitement. As our bodies thawed the realisation of what we'd achieved began to sink in and the reserved celebration of before gave way to shouting and singing.

It was one of the happiest moments of my life, to that point, but it couldnae last. There was still a four-hour bus journey home through the cold and dark and a replay to prepare for in just two nights time. Some of the lads slept on the bus but I was too excited — thinking about what we'd achieved and what it meant. A draw meant a replay at Rugby Park — all the family and friends watching. It was gaunny be huge for The Valley and I couldnae stop grinning at the prospect.

We got home at about three in the morning and, despite having just scraped a battling draw against the champions of Scotland and Europe, I still had to be up by seven to start work at the dyers.

• • •

'How was it Big Man?'

If there was one person in the whole world happier than me with the result, it was Big Tam. He couldnae get enough of it and asked me again and again how I felt when Gallagher put the ball past Leighton after my header had set him up.

'Can it not wait, Tam?' I asked him with a nervous eye on the line of vans wanting their loads, but Tam didnae give a shite.

'How was Strachan?' he wanted to know. The fact I'd played against Gordon Strachan was the thing that impressed him most. Being on the same pitch as Strachan was like being in the same bed with Jane Fonda to Tam's mind. Better, because Jane Fonda had never even played senior amateur league, let alone full professional!

'Eh, Strachan … somethin' special,' said Tam, oblivious to the angry horns going off — and this was the same man who'd dived under the bed on his wedding night when he heard thunder!

The whole Valley was buzzing. They were mostly Old Firm supporters with Killie as their occasional second team, but with Aberdeen coming to town they were all united for once — Rangers and Celtic fans arm in arm to support the locals against the Dons.

Christine's dad, Rab, was an unusual case. Grown up among lifelong Rangers fans, he'd always followed Killie, and couldnae have been prouder when his son-in-law made the side. Mind you, we only used to get about 2,000 to home games in those days. What made it worse was that Rugby Park was big enough to hold 18,000, but we hadnae seen anything like those numbers since the team's last silverware back in '66. The grand old stadium looked embarrassingly empty with just 2,000.

There was no danger of us being embarrassed though against the Dons — everyone was going and Tuesday and Wednesday at work was just a blur of excitement as I answered the same questions everywhere

At the toss before my last ever match for Killie. We were so desperate for numbers that even my boys had to play.

I went in my van. 'What was it like playing against Strachan?' 'Did we have a chance on Wednesday night?' 'Would Doug Rougvie be starring in David Attenborough's next wildlife documentary?'

I knew I was a good chance to start on the Wednesday as Bryson's broken nose would keep him out, but nothing was said at training on Tuesday night. It was only a light session — mainly to post-mortem the Monday game and talk tactics — but seriously, what sort of tactics were going to work against one of the best teams in Europe? We'd ambushed them with a late goal at Pittodrie, but these lads wouldnae take us so lightly the next time. They'd come to do a job and anything less than a six-nil defeat would be a miracle.

On the Wednesday evening, all roads led to Rugby Park. Over 6,000 were there — more than triple our usual gate — and there was an electricity snapping in the air. When assistant coach Davie Wilson tacked the team sheet to the board I was overjoyed to see my name in the starting XI, and felt ten foot tall when we went out to warm up. Christine was there, five months pregnant with our second (Stuart), with her mum and dad and all our friends. Everyone from the dyers was there and people from all the factories and businesses in the Valley. Big Tam, of course, was there front and centre in his Killie strip with his belly bulging between shirt and breeks. I couldnae stop grinning as I trotted about the park, trying to keep warm and pinching myself when I looked down the other end to where the Scottish champions were going through their well-oiled paces.

'I'm gaunny break Strachan's fuckin' leg!' laughed Coby, who like me was starting due to an injury to McDicken.

'Don't forget he's got to play for us in the World Cup,' I reminded him, who looked thoughtful in response.

'Aye, well maybe I'll just kick him up the arse a few times.'

By the time kick off rolled around I was jumping out of my skin and was quickly involved. I played out of my arse for the first 20 minutes, getting my head to everything before Rougvie, and even had a couple of shots, forcing Leighton to make saves. One shot in particular obliged the Scottish international to dive into the top left corner to turn the ball round the post and the roar from the stands was like nothing I'd ever heard before (despite having played at both Ibrox and Parkhead).

But it all started to go bad on 30 minutes. Our early domination had not produced a goal and Gordon Strachan (despite Coby's best efforts) finished a one-touch passing move with a fine shot to silence the Killie crowd. Then five minutes later they were two ahead when their captain Willie Miller put his laces through a volley from a corner. For the first time in 130 minutes of football Alex Ferguson was silent, so it's an ill wind, I suppose …

At half time, Jim Clunie was undeterred. 'There's a big crowd here tonight lads … we cannae let them down.' He gave me further instructions regarding Leighton at corners, but I was sick of getting sat on my arse so I tried something completely radical — I went for the ball. On 63 minutes we had a corner, knocked over by Jimmy Simpson, and I got up at the near post ahead of Rougvie …

Freeze frame.

The ball comes off my ear … goes onto my shoulder … loops into the air past the despairing fingertips of Jim Leighton … gently touches the back of the net.

The stands explode with passion and joy, and Killie are back in it. The lads are all over me — no Presbyterian reserve this time — and it's totally mental on the terraces. The Killie fans are all singing and the confidence surged through us like a bolt of electric blue. Alex Ferguson was on his feet screaming once again and we could finally taste the fear of our opponents. It had all been swagger and poise from the Dons but now we enjoyed the upper hand as they froze in the face of our desperate onslaught.

For a good 20 minutes we were camped around their box, I drove through tackles and got my head to crosses but nothing could get past Leighton. As the Aberdeen defence buckled he was like a man possessed, and it was him that started the movement that put the game beyond doubt. He's plucked yet another cross off my brow and then in one movement thrown the ball to Peter Weir who went haring down the touchline, got in behind our lads who were all up trying to get the equaliser, and quick as a flash we were 3 - 1 down.

With only five minutes to play, the Dons knew they'd weathered the

PLAYER PROFILE

Name . . . . LAWRIE McKINNA
Birthplace/Date . . . . . KILMARNOCK 8/7/61
Married . . . . YES
Children . . . . 2, SCOTT & STUART
Profession . . . . VAN DRIVER
Previous Club . . . . DARVEL JUNIORS
Favourite other team . . . . RANGERS
Favourite away ground . . . . SOMERSET
Favourite food . . . . STEAK
Favourite pop star U2
Favourite actor/actress . . . CLINT EASTWOOD
Favourite TV show . . . . SPORTS
TV show you switch off . . . . POLITICAL
                                    PROGRAMMES
Likes . . . . WINNING, SCORING
Dislikes . . . . SMOKING
Which person would you most like to meet . . . . .
. . . . THE QUEEN
Pre-match meal . . . . CHICKEN
Superstitions . . . . NONE
Hobbies . . . . ALL SPORTS

Photo courtesy of the Kilmarnock Standard

Snapshot of a professional footballer. Note the taste in TV programs...

storm and got all their confidence back — even started taking the piss with the fancy tricks and passes, but we didnae really mind. It was an honour just to be on the same pitch as those lads, half of whom were about to take Scotland on a successful run into the World Cup Finals in Mexico (beating Australia home and away in the process). It was no disgrace to get beaten and what a night they'd put on for The Valley!

Rougvie and Strachan shook my hand at the end, as did Alex Ferguson, who two years later would commence his epic three decades at Manchester United. Despite losing it had been a magical night, and Aberdeen went on to win both the Scottish Cup (for a third successive year) and the league, but the part-timers from Kilmarnock gave 'em one hell of a fright for 20 minutes or so.

Next morning, when I turned up to work at my usual 7.00 am, Big Tam was proud as punch in his Killie kit and his eyes were glowing like stars.

'What was it like, Big Man?' he kept asking me. 'What was it like to score against Aberdeen?'

Well, it was very satisfying. But I'd remember more fondly scoring against the cream of Scottish football if the ball hadnae come off my ear.

Scottish Cup Round 3

Monday, February 13th, 1984

Aberdeen 1 - 1 Kilmarnock

Weir 83 mins, Gallagher 90 mins

Attendance:15,000

Aberdeen: Leighton, McKimmie, Rougvie, McMaster (Porteous), McLeish, Miller, Strachan, Black, McGhee, Hewitt (Cooper), Weir.

Kilmarnock: McCulloch, McLean, Robertson, McDicken (Cockburn), Clarke, R. Clark, McGivern, McLeod, Gallagher, Simpson, Bryson (McKinna)

Referee: J. Renton (Cowdenbeath)

• • •

Scottish Cup Round 3, Replay

Wednesday, February 15th,1984

Kilmarnock 1 - 3 Aberdeen

Strachan 30 mins, Miller 35 mins, McKinna 63 mins, Weir 85 mins

Attendance: 6,101

Kilmarnock: McCulloch, McLean, Robertson, Cockburn, Clarke, R. Clark, McGivern, McLeod, Gallagher, Simpson, McKinna. Subs not used: McClurg, Cuthbertson.

Aberdeen: Leighton, McKimmie, Rougvie (Hewitt), Cooper, McLeish, Miller, Strachan, Black, McGhee, Angus, Weir. Sub not used: Porteous.

Referee: J. Renton (Cowdenbeath)

6

The Road to Wembley

By 1986 Lawrie was reasonably well established in the Kilmarnock first team.
He had a year to run on his contract and was married with two young boys.
He'd managed to buy a house in Darvel and was a big fish in the small pond
of The Valley.

But like all big fish, he was starting to wonder about other ponds …

'What the fuck have you done?'

Christine and I were sitting in the back seat of Martin Hopper's car
staring in disbelief at Wembley Park, the home ground of Box Hill in
the Victorian Premier League. There were no famous twin towers —
not even one tower. They didnae even have a wall. It was just a wire
fence with one stand that held about 300 fans. I'd left 18,000 capacity
Rugby Park for the chance to play at Wembley, in a competition I'd
never heard of at the end of the earth.

Christine repeated her question, in no mood to be polite, but we
had to make the best of the situation. After all, Martin, the president
of Box Hill FC, had paid our fares to come out to Australia. The club
was finding me a job and was also paying me $80 a week to play. It was
approximately the same deal (all things considered) as I was on back
in Scotland, but this was a whole new experience. By the age of 25 I
knew I was never gaunny make a fortune playing football in Scotland,
but I was good enough to go on adventures overseas.

This particular adventure had started when I met Willie McMillan
at the club after a game back in Kilmarnock. He'd just been on holiday
to Australia where his son Andy was playing for Box Hill and having a
great time. I'd known Andy in the lace factories and also played with

him for Darvel Juniors and Willie painted such an attractive picture about life in Australia that I found myself asking whether they might be looking for any more players.

It happened incredibly quickly. In just eight weeks we'd arranged a sports working visa, sold the house, negotiated a free transfer from Killie, said our tearful goodbyes and landed in Melbourne. Martin Hopper had picked us up and driven us straight to Wembley to admire its wide open spaces — which were more outside the ground than in. We'd come a really long way, we were jetlagged, tired and looking at a ground that no self-respecting pub team would play on back in Scotland.

I was a little bit reassured when I started training. It wisnae a bad standard and a couple of lads could certainly play. Andy was there and some other Scots: Gary McPhie, John McGinlay, Andy Hughes. I was yet to learn the importance of ethnicity to Australian football teams, but those lessons would come in due course. Box Hill was unusual in that it didnae really have an ethnic culture (unless poms and Scots and a few token Aussies constitutes a culture).

I came off the bench in my first game against Ringwood, but started the next week against Croydon City. I was standing there with Christine watching the Reserves when I saw this fancy looking bloke with slicked back hair in a denim jacket and sunglasses approaching. 'That galla* there's not Davey Logan is it?' I asked.

'And why widnae it be?' replied Christine, and sure enough he grins when he sees us. Davey was another Valley ex-pat who had emigrated a few years earlier and saw in the local paper I was gaunny be playing at Croydon. I'm happy to say that we still see Davey and his family all the time — we're godparents to his children — but that was water well short of the bridge back in '86.

I got my first Australian goal that day when Gary McPhie drove in a corner that hit an overhanging branch before deflecting to me and I nodded home at the near post. Tactical use of encroaching foliage was an aspect of the game I'd not considered back in Scotland, so it just goes to show — a professional never stops learning.

* Galla – flash bastard.

I also landed my first Australian job that week and lasted nearly a whole day. On the basis of my delivery van experience back in The Valley, I filled an opening with a lingerie company dropping off loads of bras and frilly knickers. I quite liked the idea of working in ladies' underwear but in every store the manageress handed me a feather duster and asked me to dust the ceiling. I must've been out taking a piss when they explained that part of the job description because to this day it remains a mystery to me. Was 'dust the ceiling' some sort of code — an improper suggestion for a married man perhaps? If so I must have looked a right berk when I started dusting the ceiling each time they asked, but the whole thing made me quite uncomfortable. I wanted a delivery job, not induction into some weird dusting sex cult — so I never went back.

My next job was as a night shift cleaner at Arnotts Brockhoff Biscuit Factory. It wisnae hard work — in fact it was barely work at all because the (Scottish) shop steward got right up us if we worked too fast so we had to go slowly. The job still had to be done though, so I'd get home really late and then have to train or play the next day. Eventually I solved the work problem by getting myself a delivery van and setting up as a courier. It was a good solution in theory. In practice, it meant a lad from Darvel in The Valley — a place of about 3000 people and not so many streets — was suddenly trying to find places he'd never heard of in a city of three million people. I seemed to spend my entire day with a Melways on my lap, getting a crick in my neck from looking down, which wisnae good for my football. Neither was the infamous Melbourne 'hook turn' where you can turn right only from the left lane at the busiest intersections — which makes perfect sense. I caused quite a number of 'incidents' before I got the hang of that.

I'd arrived towards the end of the season and finished with 7 goals from 10 games — which is a fair return from a striker so there was quickly interest from NSL clubs. The two pursuing me the most were Preston Macedonia and Heidelberg (who I later learned were mortal enemies, but more on that later). And once again the Scots had completely infiltrated every club. Bill Murray was the coach of Preston and the coach of Heidelberg was Roy McLaren, ex Aston Villa. I knew (and liked) Bill from back home, but it was Roy who desperately wanted a big, traditional centre-forward so he made the stronger case.

Box Hill were not allowed to sell a visa player, but Heidelberg paid $6000 'expenses' which was enough to convince them to let their new Scottish striker go after less than half a season.

• • •

'What the fuck have I done?'

It was me asking the question this time as I stared out the window at the lines of polis in riot gear keeping the fans apart. There were thousands of the bastards all singing and chanting, full of hate and adopting extremely aggressive postures towards we few, we unhappy few on the team bus. It was just like an Old Firm match except I wisnae in the crowd or watching on telly. I was directly in the way of all that passion and barely restrained violence.

Funnily enough, my first NSL game was between the two clubs chasing my signature during the off season, and this is when I really started to learn about the ethnic rivalries in Australian football. Heidelberg was a fiercely nationalistic Greek club, even though only a few of the team were Greek. Preston was a fiercely nationalistic Macedonian club and at the time there was a bit of unhappiness in the news about tensions across the border of those respective homelands. That's the old problem in a nutshell. The Australian game widnae have existed without the massive contribution of the various European nationalities displaced after the war. But the immigrants brought with them more than hopes and dreams — they brought all the old arguments that had divided them for centuries back in the old countries and what better than football as a forum for the expression of ancient grievances?

Aye, just like the Old Firm, but without the sash.

The standard of football was quite a step up from the VPL, which was reflected in the number of Socceroos in the team: Jeff Olver in goal, Alan Hunter, and Peter Tsolakis, who for some reason was known as Wee Gus⋆. The standard was also reflected in my scoring record: I

⋆ Described by one of his Scottish team mates as The Wee Gasometer, shortened to Wee Gus. (Thanks to Roy Hay for that one!)

I left 18,000 capacity Rugby Park for the wide open spaces of Wembley, Box Hill.

The car we lived in when we first came to Australia.

Trying to score against Melbourne Croatia.
That's Alan Davidson peeking through the crowd.

Giving great head for Heidelberg

got the same number of goals as the previous season but from 24 games instead of 10.

My first NSL goal came in the Greek derby against South Melbourne at Olympic Village. Stuart Stevenson (yet another Scot but playing for South Melbourne) scored an absolute bomb from 30 yards, but I got the equaliser — a left footer smashed into the top corner from the edge of the box (past Peter Laumets). The crowd went pleasingly berserk.

My most memorable game from that first NSL season was another Greek derby, at home, against Eddie Thompson's Sydney Olympic. The referee was yet another Scotsman, Donald Campbell OAM, who was a Rangers man and asked me before the game did I know how they went overnight. This was pre-internet days. The game was very physical, which was always my sort of contest. Eddie Thompson was yelling on the sideline: 'Somebody fuckin' do that big bastard!'

And I revelled in that. This was me making my mark in the NSL — a big Scottish bastard who took no prisoners and scored the occasional goal. I let every fucker know they were on the field with Lawrie McKinna and Thompson was apoplectic at the referee: 'For fuck sakes ref … get a grip of him!'

Enough was enough, and early in the second half Donald Campbell OAM sidles up to me and says: 'Sorry Big Man … one more tackle like that and you're in the book.'

'But Don …' I said, in reference to some Greek Orthodox bugger on the other side, 'he's fuckin' Catholic.'

'Is he, by God?' said Don. 'Well, one more kick then, but that's your limit.'

I played strongly in a 3 - 1 win, and the following season Eddie Thompson tried to sign me.

• • •

The money in the NSL was very different to VPL. I went from $80 a week to $400. We got paid every home game and my mate Steve Marley said to me straight after the first one: 'Come on Big Man … let's get to the front of the queue.'

59

He led me to the committee room where the club directors were sitting around a big table piled high with all the match takings. One at a time we'd go in and they'd pay us in cash, but if the crowd had been small you widnae be paid if you weren't towards the front of the queue.

Also, being of non-Greek ethnicity meant there were extra reasons to be looking out for number one — not least when it came to the Golden Boot award. Myself and Wee Gus (Peter Tsolakis) both scored seven goals for the season, but he was awarded the Golden Boot!

So I guess the moral to that story is: Beware of Greeks bearing ... erm ... just beware of any shifty buggers running a football club.

• • •

That first season for Heidelberg was a weird one, largely because the bloke who signed me (Roy McLaren) resigned before the season started on a point of principle (which no-one can afford to do anymore) and a new coach was brought in.

John Margaritis' first words to the team, on the brink of the 1987 season were as follows: 'If you're gaunny have a wank before the game, don't do it standing up because it's bad for your legs.'

Then he had a Greek Orthodox priest come in to splash water over us but I and Stuart Frazer (ex Rangers) told him we're not Catholics and we didnae want to be splashed. The team was eventually relegated at the end of that season but I dinnae believe it was because of God's disapproval of our unwillingness to receive the Greek Orthodox blessing. I do believe there was intervention, however, of the non-holy kind.

Going into the last round, we were two points ahead of Sunshine George Cross. We drew our game at St George and Sunshine played the last game of the season against our fiercest rivals, Preston Macedonia, who were coming second. Sunshine did have superior goal difference so, as long as they didn't win, we were safe.

I believe I mentioned earlier how much Heidelberg and Preston disliked each other ...

Preston suffered a lamentable lack of discipline that game and had their goalkeeper (Phil Trainedes) sent off early. Then they had another player sent off and played the second half with only nine.

Surprise, sur-fuckin'-prise. Second placed Preston got beaten by last placed Sunshine George Cross, so Heidelberg were relegated. I hadn't thought about that game for years but was reminded of it recently when I heard about that Nigerian team that was beaten 79 nil to help another club survive relegation.

• • •

Despite Heidelberg being relegated, my tally of seven goals for a team at the bottom of the league was not so bad, so APIA, Sydney Olympic and Melbourne Knights were all in for me. I was tempted to go to Sydney Olympic just for laughs after the way Eddie Thompson had abused me, but chose APIA because they were the champions and made me feel special in a way no club really had before. Rale Rasic being coach was an additional attraction. This time the 'expenses' were $10,000 for

Heidelberg, 1987: a pretty good side with several Socceroos,
including Jeff Olver, Alan Hunter and Peter Tsolakis (Wee Gus).

the arrangement. It wisnae a transfer as you werenae allowed to sell a visa player (as I still was) — but despite it not being a transfer I was no longer playing for Heidelberg.

When I flew to Sydney, I was picked up by goalkeeper Tony Pezzano in a flashy, green sports car and driven to new digs in Fivedock arranged by the club. I was pretty much dazzled by the stars in the team — besides Pezzano there was Terry Greedy, Rod Brown, Terry Butler, Arno Bertogna, Peter Tredinnick. No wonder they were champions. I was also being paid champions level wages and had been promised a $10,000 sign on fee, which was quite a lot of money in those days — enough to buy a house in some parts of Australia.

For the first few weeks I waited patiently for my ten grand. Then, when I finally asked about it, they tried to reduce it to five grand. In the end, they simply never paid. I played just the one season for APIA but it wisnae a happy time. I spent the whole season arguing about my sign on fee and it obviously affected my game as I didnae score many goals. Then Blacktown City came in for me and said they'd pay me a ten grand sign on fee, and yet another non-transfer was arranged.

But would you believe it? As soon as I was officially a Blacktown City player and asking about my sign on fee, they said: 'Why would we pay ten grand to a visa player who could leave at any moment?' They then said they would 'honour' the agreement if I became a resident. Such processes for British people were comparatively simple in those days and the club helped me through it, so before I knew it I was a permanent resident and the ten grand was duly paid.

Maybe that cash was like spinach to Popeye because I played strongly and we avoided relegation in the last game of the season.

So what the fuck had I done?

I'd become an Australian resident.

7

Power, Pain and Passion

Lawrie found himself a kind of spiritual home at Blacktown City, leaving and returning twice more (for short stints with Wollongong City and Newcastle Breakers), but his second season started with disaster.

Absolute fucking agony.

I was lying in the back of the net, where I'd landed after John Filan had leapt knees first into my ribs as I'm going for a cross.

The pain was indescribable and I'm watching through a watery blur as Jimmy Greenhall, the big Lancastrian trainer, shuffles slowly towards me with the bucket.

'Alright, lad?'

'I'm fucked, Jimmy,' I manage to gasp through gritted teeth. He signalled to the bench and the game continued without me while I was carried to the dressing room, feeling like a shark had just taken a huge bite out of my lower back.

Christine had seen me taken out and arrived in the dressing room where I'm sweating and shivering and probably in shock. A doctor arrived and said I'd have to go to hospital. So I'm driven from St George Stadium to Royal Prince Alfred, feeling every bump in the road, and soon I was lying in Casualty — writhing in agony. I couldnae have pain killers until the X-rays were done to show the doctors what they were dealing with.

'What's wrong with you, ya big soft cock?'

For a moment I was shocked that a doctor could be so unfeeling, but it wisnae the doctor. It was just my mate Darren Stewart who'd arrived to look after the kids, as it was clear I was gaunny be in for a while. As usual my friends and family were thoroughly entertained by my pain and misery so I had to put up with Darren cracking jokes about what the diagnosis and consequences were likely to be. 'It's probably just yer spinal cord snapped,' he said cheerfully. 'I doubt you'll walk again.'

Finally the X-rays showed it wisnae my spine, but it was still pretty bad — my right kidney was burst open like a cheap sausage and immediately the fear was that I might lose it. At least they were able to give me pain killer after that so I wafted away on a cloud of pethidine and didnae give a shite for about eight hours.

Increasingly the doctors were concerned though that I wisnae pissing, but as I came down off the pethidine I was able to go. It was like pissing Coca Cola there was that much blood and I started to be a bit scared. Pissing blood is not the sort of thing to fill a professional athlete with confidence.

But fear was just an occasional interlude. I spent most of the next few days spaced out on pethidine, hooked up to drips that were constantly sluicing through my system to try and clear away the damage. It was touch and go about the kidney but slowly the Coca Cola changed to Fanta and then lemon squash. The kidney was saved.

Mind you, I was not out of the woods. 'You've got to be very careful,' said the nurse. 'No excitement and no strenuous movement.'

This was in response to my request the following weekend for a day pass to go and watch the team play at Gabbie Stadium.

'The smallest knock could set you back. The kidney's not safe yet.'

I begged and pleaded and finally they gave in, really emphasising that I was not to exert myself in any way and for Christine to drive super carefully to protect me from any bumps.

We had to go home to Fivedock first, to get some clothes, and as I'm entering the house, still hooked up to my drip and bent over like Quasimodo, I suddenly felt The Urge. I'd been a week without, after all, and like any young man in his prime, I wisnae gaunny be put off by drips and damaged kidneys. 'Are you mad?' enquired Christine, but

Giving great head for Blacktown City.

Here I am nipping in with my head. The six yard box was always Lawrie Land.

A tough, traditional Scottish striker, dancing a Highland Fling while simultaneously shooting at goal.

she's only human and couldnae help but succumb to the McKinna charm. She raced out to the lounge room and bunged a cartoon video on for the boys, then dashed back to the bedroom where I was carefully assuming the position. She climbed gingerly aboard but I wisnae in my best 'Shagging for Scotland' form. It was over in seconds.

'Is that it?' cried Christine, and despite my delicate condition starts pounding into me — bucking and thrashing like there's no tomorrow. And there may well not have been had she gone on much longer!

So I'm feeling more than slightly battered and bruised when we arrive at the match an hour or so later. I had a few drinks, and then disaster — I couldnae go. I'm standing at the urinal at half time, absolutely busting, but nothing's happening.

I told Christine and immediately we're heading back to the hospital, where the nurses insisted I tell them in full detail everything that had happened between leaving and returning.

Everything.

I may not have been pissing but the medical staff were pissing themselves with laughter when we rather sheepishly admitted to having sex. But worse was to come — this stern matron was asking about the sex in very thorough detail and Christine was pink with embarrassment as the matron asked her to describe how strenuous it had been.

'Not very … ' said Christine, 'just normal.'

'No it wisnae,' I objected. 'You were trying to pound me through the mattress.'

'You were on top?' cried one of the nurses, aghast.

'There was no other way with him trussed up like a Christmas tree,' said Christine, embarrassed but defensive.

'It was dangerous and irresponsible, Mrs McKinna,' said the matron, 'Please control your urges in future.'

With that my shameless, nympho wife was ushered from the room as the medical team went into overdrive and it all got extremely uncomfortable. At first they just put me in a hot shower with a very hot water bottle to hold against my belly. That worked a little but not enough.

'We'll have to insert a catheter,' announced the matron.

'Are you taking the piss?' I asked, but they'd heard that joke before and didnae laugh. I didnae laugh either when I saw the catheter. It was like some medieval instrument of torture — a long plastic tube with three nasty-looking prongs at the end.

'Where's that going?' I asked nervously.

'You know exactly where it's going,' she said, but at least they gave me more pethidine first.

Somehow they got the thing up through my nob and into my bladder so they could start sluicing it out with water and slowly these great clots of blood start emerging from my insides.

'Don't you get any ideas,' said the nurse to Christine, who'd snuck back in.

After filling and draining my bladder several times they eventually were satisfied that the problem had been resolved, but they warned me that if I couldn't go when the catheter came out they'd have to repeat the whole process.

So next morning I'm as tense as hell as they're removing the catheter — terrified the evil looking instrument would have to be reinserted — but as it slipped out my nob went off like a fire hose all over the bed.

The relief! I've never been so happy to be lying in my own piss.

Eventually I was able to resume training but there were only four games left. I scored in my first game back and by the end of the season I felt fully restored and ready to really make my mark in Australian football.

• • •

When you're out for a while you've got too much time to think.

I was pushing 30 and pretty much at my peak as a player, and almost for the first time I found myself analysing my own game — strengths and weaknesses, playing style and strategies.

Playing up front is the hardest position of all, which is why strikers tend to get paid the most. Professional teams (usually) are well drilled at playing without the ball and rule one is stay compact. Bodies are massed between the ball and the goal and it's really hard to navigate your way through — and hardest of all for the striker who is the final cutting edge of the team weapon.

When the striker does his work he's got the least time, the least space, and facing players who are most desperate to stop him — not to mention the only bastard on the pitch allowed to use his hands. That means the striker has to develop qualities and skills to cope.

As I said at the very start I was never a gifted player. I was big, fast and strong but that disnae make a footballer. I had adequate touch, a reasonable pass, and not a bad shot. I was very good with my head (probably my best technical skill) but looking back I think what truly made me effective was the old poacher's instinct. I could get myself into good scoring positions through the sneaky little runs a striker learns to make when his marker loses concentration.

I was able to seem like I was tired, disinterested, going through the motions, and a marker would think he had me in his pocket. He switches off for a second because the ball's 40 metres away, and suddenly I'm gone.

By the time my marker thinks: 'Where the fuck's Lawrie?' it's too fuckin' late. I've nipped in at the near post for a tap in, or gone up at the far post for one of my towering headers with no bastard near me.

Being aware of my own style then made me think about the playing styles of others and how that style went with their various positions and how all of that combined to produce a team performance.

This is the very basics of team philosophy, had I known it, but from that time I was starting to prepare myself for coaching.

• • •

I went well the following season, establishing a reputation as a hard front man who could be relied upon to always cause problems for the opposition. But this was State League and I wanted to be back in the NSL.

I'd been negotiating with Manfred Schaeffer to go back to APIA and we'd agreed a verbal contract. That was the Tuesday and on the Saturday — just about the last game of the season — Manfred came to watch me play against Rockdale United.

Everything was going well until I've slid in for another of those dangerous one-on-ones with the keeper, Tony Francken. I've never pulled out of a tackle in my life (more fool me) but neither has Francken and his knee went through my tibia and fibula like a couple of celery sticks.

I thought I knew all about pain from my previous injuries. Nup ... I knew fuck all until I broke my leg. That's the real pain, and I'm lying on the ground trying not to squeal despite the excruciating agony.

Suddenly Manfred's standing over me.

'How you doing, Lawrie?' he asked, cheerfully.

'No so bad, Manfred,' I said, blinking through tears.

He checks out my leg and says: 'I don't talk to ex-players.' And the bastard walked away! I laughed, knowing it was just his brutal German sense of humour, but I never went back to APIA. In fact, it was 22 months before I played first team again for anyone.

When I first tried to come back, about nine months later, well into the following season, I was still limping but trying to hide it. My third game in the Reserves, I knew I wisnae hitting my straps, and each game my leg was hurting more. Finally I admitted what everyone else was telling me — the leg was killing me. So I had a quiet word with Jimmy.

'Have you got something you can give us for the pain?'

'Aye,' he says and brings out his magic bag of tricks. I thought he was gaunny give me a jab, but he reaches down into my sock and smears my leg with this red goop which immediately started to burn.

'What's that gaunny do for my leg?' I asked.

'Fuck all,' said Jimmy, 'but it'll burn like hell and take your mind off the injury.'

He was dead right. I got through the game but subsequent X-rays showed there were still hairline fractures all through my leg. The result was another year out of the game. This time I did a proper rehabilitation (while studying for my coaching badges) and when I came back for the last part of the 1991 season I got ten goals in as many games. Once again I was ready to sign for an NSL club and really make my mark.

• • •

The next time back I broke my jaw.

It was a semi-final against Canberra and three minutes in I went up for a header with their big defender Dunn. He's 'dunn' me alright — absolutely tanned my jaw for me and I was that incensed I spent most of the match squaring up with him. I did briefly pause from my vengeance to get two goals in a 3 - 2 win, so despite the pain that was a very satisfying result.

When I came off my jaw was killing me and I could barely open my mouth, and when I looked in the mirror it was like I had two heads. The whole side of my face was swollen and Jimmy Greenhall said: 'Looks like fracture, lad.'

Jimmy's diagnosis was confirmed by a surgeon the following day, and he recommended I have an operation immediately. Well that wisnae gaunny work as it would have meant me missing the Grand Final against Bankstown.

We booked the operation for the Monday after the GF and just kept the injury secret — not that Bankstown would have deliberately taken advantage of my pain and tried to injure me further …

It didnae matter. I hit the bar with a speculator in the first half but that's as close as we came to scoring. Yet another one goal loss in a Grand Final — surely I'd had my fill of those!

The following night I was lying in hospital after my operation and couldnae sleep with the pain, so I turned on the telly and got to watch Sydney announced as the Olympic City for 2000.

Despite missing a lot of games through injury those were very successful years for me. From 1991 to 1993 I got 25 goals in 39 games. But injuries, and time on the side line ... Aye, too much time to think.

I knew my playing days were drawing to a close.

8

One Door Closes ...

There comes a time in every player's career when the curtain must come down. Lawrie hung on for Blacktown — still scoring goals when on the park — but injuries made his appearances fewer and further between.

Always a pragmatist, he knew that if he wanted to stay in the game (and he certainly did) then he'd have to find some new skills.

When I broke my leg, the first grade coach was Ken Schembri and the Youth Team coach was Kelly Cross who defended Ken when attacked one day by an angry Greek gentleman. Kelly sits him on his arse and gets suspended. So, being unable to play at the time, I took over the reserves and we went really well and made it to the finals. And my reward? Dumped as soon as Kelly was allowed back — which was fair enough.

That experience gave me quite an interest in coaching and about then NSW Soccer started a Zone Program for new coaches run by Steve O'Connor (including John Kosmina and Joe Watson). There were some top young players involved in the program, which was where I first met Kwas (Adam Kwasnik), Mark Bridge and Ivan Necevski.

So what did I learn?

Not a whole lot about football but a hell of a lot about politics: dealing with players, dealing with parents, other coaches and especially administrators. It's all politics and you've got to learn how to wheel and deal your way through competing or conflicting views and motives. Does your head in but if you've not got the stomach for it, don't bother trying to be a professional coach.

The other thing I learned was the importance of planning and preparation. Every match and every training session you've got to make sure that everything's all set up and ready for when the players arrive. Training sessions in particular need to be all planned out so you're not standing about and scratching your head when players ask what you're doing and why.

I wisnae that good at explaining why in those days but later I learned how important it was — especially to professional players who've come through the ranks and done every kind of training drill known to man. They'll just go through the motions if you don't explain why they're doing it and what they're supposed to get out of it.

• • •

First insight into coaching

Players need to understand the point of training drills. I always liked high intensity drills that forced players to use their skills and make decisions under pressure. A three-on-one grid is perfect for this as it forces players to trap and pass while being constantly closed down, use their vision, move to open up passes for others and, most importantly, to plan two passes ahead. They get good at this and can use the same skills to manoeuvre in triangles into good positions during games.

But the key is time. You've got to explain to the players that what they're trying to do is maximise time on the ball for the man furthest from the piggy-in-the-middle trying to close them down. Once they translate that to a game they're creating time for a player to do something to hurt the opposition. The most precious commodity in football is time — especially in front of goal.

Once the players understand the point of what they're doing they'll get into it with more enthusiasm, work harder and benefit more from the drill than if they're thinking: 'What the fuck are we doing this for?'

• • •

My first coaching gig. John McDonald is second left – lovely bloke.

Left: Me and Kostya Tszyu
at Parramatta Stadium.
The photo was taken
just moments before
he spilled my pint.

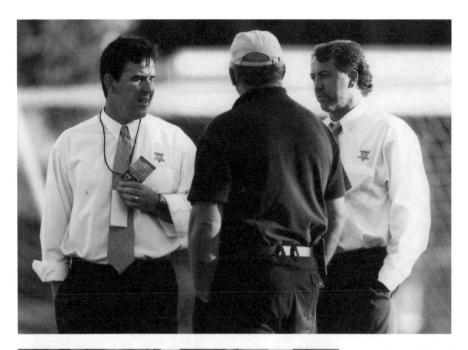

Above: Me and
Davie Mitchell – a
great team. I learned
a lot from him.

The biggest cheque
I ever received in
professional football.

Speaking of time, this was when I really started to know that mine was up, as a player, so was pretty interested in any opportunity to start coaching. I was invited by John McDonald (lovely man and excellent football coach) to play for Hills United in the state league, on the condition that I become player-coach the following year. I was happy to accept, but imagine how I felt at my first training session when a fellow introduced himself as Danny Abboud, reserve team coach, and told me he'd be head coach next year. It didnae turn out that way, and I've occasionally run into Danny around the football traps, so I'm glad he stayed in the game.

When I did become head coach myself I was paid a few hundred dollars a game and at the time was employed by Asics who sponsored the club (Asics first ever sponsorship of a football team in Australia) for ten grand, which more than covered my wages.

That was a great year — a terrific bunch of boys and we did well. In all honesty, my coaching would have been fairly basic in those days so I don't claim a lot of credit. Nevertheless, coaching is so much about the subtleties of leadership, which is all about understanding your team both as individuals and collectively. If you don't get that you'll never have success, no matter how many coaching badges you've got.

• • •

Second insight into coaching

Professional coaching is as much about man management as it is about football strategy and systems, so understand your players both individually and collectively.

Understand how a team works: its motives, desires and fears. Learn how to press its buttons and when to leave it alone.

The same goes for the individuals. Understand how they operate as human beings within a team structure and how those individuals fit with the specific roles required of each position within your system. Also understand how each player responds to and learns from criticism. One of the biggest mistakes new coaches tend to make is trying to treat everyone the same. People are different. Politicians and judges may have to treat everyone the same but not coaches. It's a football team not a fucking democracy, so a successful coach is like a benevolent dictator who is loved by his players for his ability to understand them and treat them as they individually and collectively need.

• • •

Anyway, I was still more of a sporting goods salesman than a football coach back then, but one day David Barrett from Sydney Olympic came in to pick up his Asics Testimonials. I asked him, who's your coach? He said Davie Mitchell's got the job (who I'd played against when he was playing for Rangers).

'Who's his assistant?'

'He's not got one, give him a call.'

So I phoned him up and blew my own trumpet very loudly, which isnae really my style, but Mitch said: 'That all sounds fine but I've just offered the job to Terry Butler, although he hasn't accepted yet. There might be an issue with his work. I'll call you back.'

An hour later he called back and to my great joy said: 'Can you be at training this afternoon?'

So I met him at training at Belmore and we hit it off immediately. We both had the same piss-taking sense of humour and it was like we were old friends rather than two arseholes who'd occasionally kicked the crap out of each other in Scotland. We went on a fantastic run getting crowds of 12,000 and more at Belmore and just missed the finals after coming from the bottom of the league when Mitch and I took over. Unfortunately, however, the first team coaching job had already been offered to Geoff Harcombe for the following year, so despite our success we were out the door.

But one door closes and another opens. The Dynamic Duo of Mitchell and McKinna were offered the job together at Sydney United. We won the league in '97 and made the Grand Final against South Melbourne.

The scandal from that game was that in the lead up to the GF the club said they wanted us to come back straight after for the fans at King Tomislav Club, but our families had already booked their flights to come with us (and back home with us). We didn't want to be rushed back — especially if we lost as there'd be two men and a dog at the club. But the club were insistent and the players equally adamant. The captain, Velemir Kupresak, appealed to the club: 'Come on farken … we're here to play football farken!'

Then Joe Moric said: 'Okay, I'll go back to Sydney.'

That was enough to satisfy honour on both sides so the game went ahead. We got done 3 - 2, Joe was whisked away to the airport to go back to Sydney with the club officials to commiserate at the club with the fans — both of them and their dog, a Labrador, I believe.

So, that was my first Grand Final loss as a coach. There were plenty more to follow.

• • •

Third insight into coaching

I was still very much learning the basics but at Sydney United under Mitch I learned that getting the best out of the players was all about making them enjoy their work.

That's where I realised how my coaching style was gaunny develop — high tempo, enjoyable, fun. We were playing small-sided games and the banter was flowing, the goals were going in, the players were working hard and loving it. A light bulb moment.

• • •

At the end of that first successful season (with Mitch winning NSL Coach of the Year), the club rewarded us by offering us less money to go round again the next season. One of the main sponsors (in the shadowy background) offered me a large amount of cash to do the dirty on Mitch and take over the team, which I accepted with great enthusiasm.

Like fuck I did.

An extremely happy and successful club was suddenly in crisis due to the ingratitude and skulduggery of certain directors. And then, out of nowhere, Parramatta Power appeared.

They were putting their own new club together and Dennis Fitzgerald flashed his great big cheque book at us. Sydney United had been told that Power widnae be let in but Soccer Australia never had much money and couldnae resist. So the Sydney United club — who'd just won the league, made the Grand Final, and offered the coaches and players less money to do it all again — watched us all troop across the road to Parramatta Power who were, in a way, an A-League club in the old NSL. The set up was totally professional and made you feel like a professional instead of a part-timer. (And we were part-timers most of us — I'd only just left Asics at that time.)

The Sydney United fans never forgave us, but they didnae understand the reason (and didnae have to pay our mortgages). The first time we went back to King Tom, Mitch and I were deliberately last out onto the pitch and were booed during the national anthem. After the game we were spat on, shouted at, had cups of piss thrown at us — made me quite nostalgic for Scotland.

Then in 2000, back at King Tom, we were getting abused again and Christine had a go at some arsehole in the crowd. Then the guy said: 'Have you ever been raped, Mrs McKinna? Because we know where you live … Brampton Drive, Kellyville.'

Christine shut her mouth, for about the first time in her life, but she was truly scared — and this was the days before iPhones so she couldnae take a picture of the cunt for the polis. On reflection, I'd realised I'd done some coaching clinics for a sponsor who, in return, had given me a great deal on some air conditioning, which had been installed by Sydney United fans. That's possibly why everyone knew our address.

We were at Power for three seasons and the club was fantastic, but we probably didnae do quite well enough and they didnae renew our contracts. Mind you, I retain the highest respect for Dennis Fitzgerald who was always completely honest with us. I suspect that Parramatta

Davie Mitchell and I were very successful at Sydney United,
but not enough to be paid the same wages the following season.

Off to see the mighty Gers with my brother-in-law, Jim Grimley,
playing a traditional air flute.

Me agreeing 100% with the referee.

Leagues could do with his leadership even now.

After five years with Davie Mitchell I was getting to the stage where I was having my own ideas and wanting to give them free rein. I'd learnt a heap from Mitch but eventually the time comes when you must become your own man or you'll never develop further.

And that's when Spirit approached me.

• • •

Fourth insight into coaching

The coach has to be the boss.

• • •

I was finding my feet at that time — first time as a senior coach — so naturally all the players were testing me out to see where my limits were. Players will always do this at any level so you need to establish the ground rules early.

At one of my first Northern Spirit training sessions, Michael Cartwright, a big defender, gave me a chance to establish the Lawrie McKinna Way when he questioned my decision in a short-sided game. He mouthed off, trying to see how far he could push the first time coach.

'Shut your fuckin' mouth or I'll fuckin' shut it for you,' I suggested, quite reasonably I think. But he mouthed off again under his breath so I went at him. Told him to fuck off and I'd see him in my office later. After that, the boys realised I was serious and it got a lot easier.

Having said that, you can't just explode every time some lippy bugger disagrees with you. It's all about proportionality and building relationships. A coach and his team spend so much time together — more than you spend with your family during the season. It can get quite claustrophobic. And all those young footballers with too much time on their hands and very much focused on the coach (I hope) will start to analyse and press buttons. Therefore you've got to know yourself and your own sensitivities much better than the players do, because footballers are ruthless. A coach without the strength of character to put up with footballers taking the piss is not destined for the big league.

I was mostly on very friendly terms with all my players over the years and that Cartwright incident was almost the only time I ever had to get aggressive. He was quite apologetic about his behaviour and I apologised for my aggressive response, and then we were best of mates.

But while I was learning a hell of a lot about being a professional coach, it wisnae a happy time at Spirit. These were the death throes days of the NSL when there was no money in the game and little mainstream interest. The Socceroos having lost to Iran in '97 and then to Uruguay in 2001 were at their lowest ebb and you widnae even put the game on life support. The merciful thing would have been to just put a pillow over its face and let it go, but somewhere or other the Crawford Report was commissioned and, while I would never have believed it at the time, better days were ahead.

9

Thieves and Billionaires

Historians suggest that the final days of the old NSL were very like Germany at the end of the war. The major powers jockeyed amid the chaos for position in the post-conflict world while a multitude of victims were forced overseas or tried to rebuild their lives from the rubble.

Germany was like that also.

Lawrie McKinna was coach of Northern Spirit at the end of the NSL, but as his world collapsed around him he read the Crawford Report and heard rumours of a new football ready to rise from the ashes.

But, as Lawrie says: 'The phoenix disnae always rise. Sometimes it just burns.'

When Northern Spirit exploded into life in 1998 they regularly had crowds of 16,000 plus at North Sydney Oval. But only five years later we were struggling to survive — playing at Pittwater Park in front of a handful of fans as the NSL writhed on its post-Crawford death bed.

In the very last days, money was non-existent. Some of the boys were living in the club-arranged digs at Warriewood and always under threat of eviction because, while the club was supposed to be docking rent from their wages, it was rarely passed on to the real estate agents.

Not that there usually were any wages in the first place. Things were so bad that some of the boys resorted to thieving bread from the local supermarket. There were cars repossessed and marriages under stress — it was nearly as bad as playing professional football in Scotland! Sometimes I'd turn up to training and the team were all so starved and wretched I'd say: 'Bugger this ... we're back to mine for a barbie. Youse bring the bread.' And I only had money myself because I had set up a delivery business with my boys.

On more than one occasion the council locked us out of the training pitch for non-payment of rent, and we nearly didn't get to play our last ever game which was to be Alex Tobin's retirement. The former Socceroo captain, with more caps and NSL appearances than any other player, was about to be denied his final bow because the club owed money and the receivers couldnae carry on. How many other football codes in Australia would allow a player of such distinction to be treated so shabbily?

Well, fortunately it didn't quite come to that. A new consortium — the Spirit Sports and Leisure Group owned by Brian Sewell, Andrew Sylvester and Jerry Raterman — generously came to the rescue, putting up $160,000 just so the final game could go ahead. Alex Tobin and long-serving goalkeeper Paul Henderson got to say their goodbyes and received standing ovations from the three and a half thousand who watched our last ever game against Adelaide United.

I was proud we were able to give the boys some kind of send-off but deeply disappointed the league had finished up after coming out from Scotland to be part of it. Of course, I hadnae been paid myself for a long time so, despite the rumours of the new A-League setting up, the idea of making my living from football was about as realistic as winning the lottery.

Nevertheless, the new consortium was determined to put in a bid for one of the precious A-League licences and they wanted me on board as their inaugural coach and also as a lobbyist. I still wisnae paid anything but, while continuing to run my delivery business, I found myself chasing a pipe dream — attending meetings all over Sydney, night after night, to help establish the credentials of the Spirit Sports and Leisure Group as a viable proposition in the new football world.

Transferring Northern Spirit up to Gosford was the basic plan, but the financial underpinning for such a venture was a guarantee of about $4 million per year. Where on earth were Sewell, Sylvester and Raterman gaunny find that sort of money?

The answer was Lyall Gorman, a wealthy magnate with decades

of success in sport-related business. They lobbied him to come on board and when he eventually took over the finances (with the Spirit Sports and Leisure Group effectively shunted aside for 5% of the new entity) the prospects of the Central Coast Mariners were dramatically improved.

The first time I ever saw Lyall was on the telly on Melbourne Cup Day in 2004 when the announcement came through that the Mariners were to be one of the eight inaugural clubs in the A-League. And almost beyond my wildest dreams I received a call the next day from Lyall asking me to meet him at his office in the city.

I left immediately, collecting Ian Ferguson along the way, and we soon found ourselves in a different world. In Lyall's office it was like money was oozing out of the walls and at last I felt that just maybe there was some kind of substance to the old promise of Australian football. I was very happy to know that people like Lyall existed and were prepared to invest in the game. He wanted me on board as the Central Coast Mariners inaugural coach for three years at $100k per season. How did I feel about that?

Fucking brilliant, at the time, even though I'd not consulted an agent to try and get some idea of what the market was paying. I later discovered I was by some distance the lowest paid head coach in the league. We shook hands on the deal and Lyall said he'd get something drawn up in the next few days.

I started work at once, with Ian Ferguson and Alex Tobin as assistants. The contract didnae materialise but on the 15th of November my first pay cheque arrived. Well, that was good enough for me and I continued feverishly putting together the building blocks of a brand new football club. The first to sign on was Damien Brown, soon followed by others I'd worked with in the bad old days at Spirit: Stuart Petrie, John Hutchinson, Adam Kwasnik, Noel Spencer, Alex Wilkinson.

The players were starting work on the 1st of March but the coaching staff were already hard at it, and hardly noticed when the December pay cheque never arrived.

Neither did the January cheque, nor the February, but I was so used to never getting paid in Australian football, and so excited about starting work with the players in March, that I wisnae too bothered, and whenever I spoke to Lyall he'd reassure me about both the money and the contract.

I was also distracted by the buzz. The excitement behind the dawn of the A-League, which was to be shown live on TV by Foxtel, was unparalleled in Australian domestic football. With the exception of Adelaide United and Perth Glory all the teams were brand new, and yet supporters for the new clubs were coming out of the woodwork — already in love with teams that barely existed on paper.

Well, the Mariners were a bit more than paper, but not a lot more. We had a tiny office at Mingara Sports Club at Tumbi Umbi which was also our first training base. When the players first assembled they were blown away by the facilities that looked suspiciously like proper professional facilities. They were even fed lunch after training every morning at the Chinese buffet. It was paradise!

Finally I was paid again on the 15th of March (no back pay mind). From that time on I was always paid in the middle of the month, but whenever I asked about my contract I was told it'd be sorted out shortly. I was starting to get a little uncomfortable on that score but with the regular pay cheques now coming in and the excitement about the start-up of the A-League I never pressed too hard.

The first competitive matches we played were the World Club Championships qualifying tournament in May 2005, and from the very start the Mariners punched above their weight — something, I'm proud to say, we've always done and still do … mostly. We had the smallest population catchment and the least resources, but we had the community behind us and we built a spirit in the team that went way beyond the cobbled together stars of the glamour clubs. That spirit took us to the final of the tournament, won by Sydney FC, who went on to win the Oceania Champions League and then play against Saprissa (CONCACAF*) and Al Ahly (CAF**) in Japan.

Those were the stakes we were now playing for and as we got closer

* Confederation of North, Central American and Caribbean Association Football
** Confederation of African Football

to the season proper, the buzz was so huge I was always too distracted to worry about minor details like contracts or my family's financial security.

Then came the inaugural A-League Pre-season Cup — and we've gone out and won it, beating Glory 1 - 0 in the final. Could this Lawrie McKinna felly coach or fuckin' what?

That's the time I first started to pressure Lyall for a written contract. A coach is always strongest after winning a trophy so amid all the celebration in the dressing room I found a quiet moment to collar Lyall and as usual he slapped me on the back and said his people would have it sorted in days.

Well it wisnae sorted.

The months rolled by, the Mariners did well — always within striking distance of the league leaders — and I started to come up with some theories as to why I wisnae worth a contract in writing. The League was new, and despite the immediate success was not guaranteed to survive beyond the novelty honeymoon period. Massive injections of cash were needed to keep the teams afloat and it finally occurred to me that if the league collapsed inside three years, Lyall could be personally liable for the balance of my contract, plus the contracts of my staff. But that was a drop in the bucket compared with the rest of the costs of running the club so that hypothesis didnae make sense. And I want to be fair to Lyall, for all the mystery of how my contract was managed, there's no doubt that he did a great job for the Mariners. In fact they widnae have existed without him.

Sometime during that first season, John Singleton came onto the board of the FFA*. He was the head licensee of Bluetongue Stadium so had a massive interest in the success of the Mariners, and not just for his own business. Singo loves the Coast to bits and will support anything that can raise its profile. He's naturally a rugby league man but fell in love with football when he saw what it was doing to make the Central Coast Mariners such a positive community focus and symbol of underdog success throughout Australia.

* Football Federation Australia

He started coming into the rooms after matches and was quickly popular with the boys. He'd have us out to his place for barbies and we became good mates. When I mentioned my contractual situation he thought it totally bizarre, but none of his business.

I think it was the week of the Grand Final I was asked at a press conference about my contract. In front of a packed room of journalists I replied that I didnae have a contract, nothing on paper at least. Lyall was contacted about this and wisnae pleased. He told the press that the Mariners had an 'agreement' with Lawrie, and quickly after he finally offered me something in writing.

But quite a lot had changed by that time.

I was now in a much stronger bargaining position, not just because of the outstanding success of the Mariners, the success of football in general was off the scale. The Socceroos had just overturned 32 years of heartache and were about to go to Germany; the A-League had smashed all expectations in its first year; there were rumours of a massive new deal in the works with Foxtel to underwrite the league. The survival of the league was guaranteed (at least for the next few years). Lyall was certainly going to need a coach so why not keep the quite successful one he already had?

A contract, on real paper and everything, was placed in front of me.

'Fuck off,' I said to Lyall. 'I'm not signing this.'

'Why not?'

The contract was more or less what we had originally agreed: $100k per year for the first three seasons but no increase or bonuses. And by that time I had an idea what the other (less successful) coaches were getting and, therefore, what Lawrie McKinna was worth.

'I've been asking for a contract for over 12 months and you want me to sign now? When I'm totally focused on the Grand Final? I'm not signing anything until after the dust settles and I've had time to think.'

Well, as we all know, the Mariners lost the Grand Final to Stevie Corica's shot from Dwight Yorke's set up at a sold out Sydney

Football Stadium. A magnificent occasion to end the inaugural season and, despite the loss, the tributes flowed in for the team that had done so much with so little. And also for the coach. I was deeply humbled to receive the A-League's first Coach of the Year award, but also interested to hear the rumours that Pierre Littbarski was not seeing eye to eye with the board at Sydney FC after winning the first Grand Final.

Shortly afterwards it came out that Sydney had lost around $6 million in the first season and, to reward Littbarski for his success, they asked him to accept a 50% reduction in salary. For some odd reason he refused, and I was surprised to receive a phone call from Leo Karis — football agent to the stars. He knew I hadn't signed a contract with the Mariners and wanted to know would I go with him to meet Walter Bugno, chairman of Sydney FC, to talk about the Sydney job. This was the day before Littbarski announced he was leaving Sydney.

The next thing I know I'm being feted at Walter's eye-popping mansion and being promised the world. We spoke about a two year deal: $170k (less than a quarter of what they'd been paying Littbarski) per season plus big performance bonuses. That was more money than I had ever dreamed of making in football, plus the incredible facilities enjoyed by Sydney FC, and all of it actually written down on paper. They were pressing me to make a decision straight away and it was doing my head in because I loved the Coast. Not just the football club, I was happily settled in a community that had really embraced me and Christine so it would be quite a wrench to leave that. But I wisnae being looked after.

So back at home, Christine and I are talking it over, and I think I'd pretty well made up my mind to take the Sydney job when the phone rings again.

'You're not goin' anywhere ya big Scottish cunt!'

'Erm … excuse me, who is speaking?'

'It's Singo! I'm comin' to your fuckin' house right now and you're signing a contract with me!'

He'd obviously had a few so I told him I'd meet him at Iguana Joe's which was his favourite local watering hole.

'I'm comin' right now!' he slurred. 'Make sure you're there or I'm comin' to your fuckin' house!'

There's no arguing with billionaires so I went to Iguana's, a Gosford watering hole that would later become famous for other reasons, and waited for Singo who was coming from North Sydney — hopefully not driving himself. Suddenly there's a screeching of tyres as an old station wagon careers into the car park and Singo just about falls out of the passenger seat and thrusts a phone at me.

It's John O'Neill (CEO of the FFA) on the phone who says the deal with Sydney is off. I eventually learn that Singo got wind of the Sydney offer and immediately rang Frank Lowy (on holiday in Tel

Littbarski was an excellent coach but abandoned the Sydney job just because they wanted to halve his wages. Well boohoo. (*Daily Telegraph*, March 2006)

Aviv) to tell him to leave Lawrie alone or he'd tell the press Lowy was using his influence to favour Sydney FC at the expense of the league. Frank Lowy, chair of the FFA, was always extremely sensitive to any suggestion he might be favouring Sydney, so he was straight onto John O'Neill to tell him Lawrie McKinna was not to be tampered with. O'Neill was obviously amused by the turn of events and told me to get every cent I could out of Singo, whose bargaining position was not exactly strong after such a passionate display. Wouldnae mind playing him at poker.

So we troop into Singo's back office at Iguana's and start to negotiate, writing down the details on the back of a Mother's Day lunch menu. He offered me five years at $175k per year, plus performance bonuses. The way it worked was that I'd still (with Leo Karis) be negotiating with Lyall Gorman, but anything I couldn't get directly from the Mariners would be made up personally by Singo (who was also sponsoring the club for a very substantial amount of money). He undertook to pay out the entire contract, even if the club folded!

Lyall was not impressed when he learned what had happened and clearly felt himself to be under pressure to agree to (more or less) the same terms, so in the end it didn't cost Singo a cent and I was really happy to be staying on the Coast. Within a few days I finally signed a contract with Lyall Gorman, but there's no way I would've got such favourable terms without Singo's intervention.

So I finally had a contract, after all that effort and all the crap I'd put up with since the bad old days at Spirit. I hadnae been just coach to those boys but also caterer, bodyguard, banker, nursemaid, confidante and just plain friend, somehow holding it all together despite a total lack of money and the often inscrutable behaviour of the many conflicting personalities that make up professional football.

When I made my speech accepting my Coach of the Year award, I was tempted to talk about the trials and tribulations that had, against all rhyme and reason, brought the Mariners to where they were — a new byword for achievement against the odds in Australian sport. But instead I limited myself to what the punters wanted to hear on such an auspicious occasion. Aye, I was humbled to have won the award ... I wanted to thank the fans and the boys, and of course the CEO of the

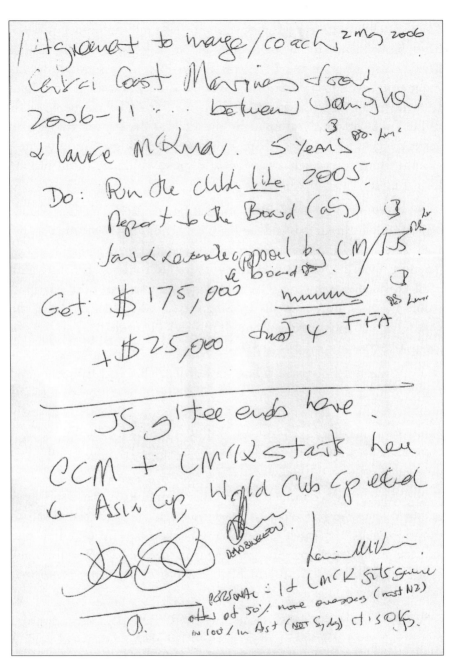

Iguana Joe's Mothers' Day menu, complete with my contract details. As agreed with
Singo, I was promised five years and the Barramundi.

Mariners, Mr Lyall Gorman, for his unswerving support.

Lyall gave us a big smile and the crowd all politely applauded as I held up my trophy. But they didnae know the half of it.

10

Heaven & Hell

In Year One of the A-League — or Version One as it was called at the time — a new breed of marketer promoted a new breed of footballer. Spiky-haired Chad Gibson (complete with diamond stud ear ring) looked very cool indeed as he dipped a football in paint and kicked it against a wall to spell out the new A-League logo.

It is a staggering piece of A-League history that the Mariners — or Rag-arse Rovers as Lawrie called his beloved team — did so well against the powerhouses arrayed against them. Just the fact that the Mariners were even in the competition was amazing. The fact that they almost won it was nothing short of miraculous.

From the moment I was appointed coach I was building the team. With my assistants Fergie and Alex Tobin we were constantly talking about the team we were trying to put together and the way we wanted to play. I very quickly had some of my old Spirit boys in place like Hutch, Wilko and Stuart Petrie, but we knew we needed some quality X factor-type players. I was delighted to sign Tom Pondeljak but the one I really wanted (bearing in mind the Mariners very limited salary cap) was Andre Gumprecht — brought up in the old East German football academy and an outstanding player by Australian standards.

I knew others were chasing him but it was Christine's cooking that got him over the line. He had no relatives in Australia, so we invited him up for Christmas lunch in December 2004. He quite liked the set up I showed him and loved the turkey, so signed on the spot. I started to feel just a little bit of confidence — you sign one top-line player and others will suddenly take you more seriously.

The Mariners first turned up for work on 1st of March 2005 at the Mingara Sports and Leisure Centre at Tumbi Umbi, and no-one had a clue who we were. We might have been a troop of travelling salesmen for all the excitement we caused, but never mind. They'd soon find out about us.

The captain was Noel Spencer and the squad included Nigel Boogaard, John Crawley, Leo Carole, Russell Woodrough, Andrew Clark★, Paul O'Grady, Alex Wilkinson, Matthew Osman, John Hutchinson, Danny Vukovic, Wayne O'Sullivan, Michael Beauchamp, Andre Gumprecht, Dean Heffernan, Adam Kwasnik, Tom Pondeljak, Nick Mrdja, Stuart Petrie and Fergie as emergency player and assistant coach. John Crawley was also goalkeeping coach, his main contribution as he had a career ending injury in one of the first games, so Vuka was first choice by the time the season rolled around.

It was a stinking hot day and the boys were excited by the facilities and the professional training gear provided by the FFA, but that excitement was nothing compared to how they felt when they realised they got free access to the all-you-can-eat Chinese bistro every lunchtime. Fuckin' paradise. The boys hoed in like starving mongrels, ripping and snatching, their ravenous muzzles streaked with fried rice and hoi sin sauce …

Paradise lasted about a week, after which they couldnae face the idea of a single dim sim. So I had to make alternative and substantially healthier arrangements, including with some local businesses who still sponsor the Mariners to this very day.

Our first preparation was for the World Club Championship — an interesting prospect for a club in the very first blush of existence. We'd have to win the A-League knock-out competition to qualify for the Oceania competition (Australia was still in Oceania until the end of 2006). If we won that we were off to Japan to take on the Champions of Europe and South America. Piece of piss.

After a month of full time professional training, our first ever trial, on 30th March, was against Gladesville Spirit. We were depressingly

★ Doubling as fitness coach, which meant we could keep part of his salary outside the cap. Not that we ever went anywhere near reaching the cap.

clunky and I don't even remember the score. Things improved a few days later when we played Wyoming Tigers — the local Central Coast Premier League champions. It was still pretty clunky and we only led 1 - 0 at half time, but then the full time professional fitness clicked into gear and we ran away with it in the second half, playing glorious football and finishing nine goals up.

Our next trial was much tougher, against Manly United who were well into their season in the NSW State League. It was a bit of a setback as we struggled to a 3 - 3 draw. A week or so later we beat Blacktown City 3 - 0 in a polished performance, and then finished our pre-tournament preparation with a solid 2 - 0 result over Bonnyrigg White Eagles.

After that, all roads led to Bluetongue for the World Club Championship and our first competitive games against A-League opposition. I honestly didn't have a clue how we'd go.

Reasonably well, as it turned out. Our first game was against Newcastle Jets and finished 0 - 0 but we went through on penalties, which told me something about the mental strength of my team. Unfortunately, Nick Mrdja broke Andrew Durante's leg in that game, and that's not the only thing that snapped — any possible goodwill there might have been between our two clubs was gone forever.

In the semi we comfortably beat Adelaide United 4 - 2. We were clearly the fitter team and guys like Pondeljak and Gumprecht were really showing their class.

Then the final against Sydney FC. Christine was really excited about the prospect of going to the Oceania tournament in Tahiti so it was up to me to deliver. It was a really tight game, which I think we probably shaded on the balance of play but David Carney hit a total screamer from 25 metres and that remained the difference. It was the first game we'd ever lost and while I was disappointed, it was nothing compared to Christine's disappointment. 'Thanks a fucking lot!' she said when I got home. 'What about my ten days in Tahiti?'

I didnae get any for a month, but that was the least of my problems.

Because my next problem was Celtic.

. . .

We'd been invited to Hong Kong for a sevens tournament (on astro-turf), and in our group was Glasgow Celtic — the team I'd grown up loathing and despising from my earliest days in The Valley.

We were watching them train the day before the tournament started and they were like gods the way they knocked the ball around. Then we went out for our session and looked like a bunch of amateurs (with the Celtic players chuckling on the sideline). We couldnae control the A-League balls on the astro-turf and I thought: 'We're gaunny get smashed at this rate.'

I had to get the players' confidence up so I stopped the session and managed to find another astro-turf pitch where no-one was watching. I also managed to pinch a couple of the special balls that were being used in the tournament and hey presto! All of a sudden we looked like Barcelona! That got the boys happy again, but not for long. In the first game we were beaten by the Hong Kong Chairman's XI. We bounced back to beat Hong Kong, which meant that in our final game against Celtic, we just needed a draw to go through.

In the end, I reckon that first training session where we couldnae control the ball probably helped us. Celtic maybe took us too lightly because they never troubled us and we held on for a 0 - 0 draw and went through at their expense. They werenae chuffed about it, but it was a great day for a Rangers fan. For an encore, we beat Manchester United 2 - 1 in the quarters, which got reported in the news back in Scotland. My sister rang from back home and said: 'Did I just see on the telly that you've beaten Man United in Hong Kong?'

'It was only their reserves,' I said, 'but aye.'

'That's incredible!' she said.

And it was. We lost the semi to PSV Eindhoven but by God we'd put the Central Coast on the world stage. It may have been only a pre-season sevens tournament but some good teams were there, and plenty of good judges.

Next it was the Pre-season Cup and we capped a successful tournament by beating Perth Glory 1 - 0 in the final, our first silverware.

By this time I was convinced that with Fergie and Alex I'd built a team that was gaunny do the Central Coast proud in the A-League.

• • •

Our A-League debut was against Perth at Members Equity Stadium on a Friday night — the much anticipated season opener after the longest pre-season in Australian football. Eleven thousand people turned up and got to see the best goal of the season. Steve McMahon (ex-Liverpool) was their coach and we had a running battle all night on the sideline.

He was a seriously passionate man. When Stuart Petrie went down injured and we kicked the ball out, one of their players subsequently threw it back to us and copped a massive bollocking from McMahon for giving aid and comfort to the enemy.

The game was decided by Noel Spencer's bomb from 35 metres. It was an unbelievable strike — one of the best I've ever seen — and the joy of the players at the goal, and then again at the final whistle was truly uplifting. They all ran to the bench clustering in delight with the other players and the coaching staff and it was in moments like that the famous Mariners spirit was born.

Spirit came to the fore again in the fourth game of the season away to Dwight Yorke's Sydney FC. We came from behind to win with a freakish goal when Spencer's 91st minute free kick hit Ceccoli's shoulder, spun high into the air and took a wicked spinning bounce to deceive Clint Bolton. Once again the whole team came racing over in the pouring rain and sliding into the bench. Our bond was now so strong we didn't care who we played. We knew we could beat them.

• • •

Fifth insight into coaching

Keeping my cool. Despite the early success and excellent team spirit we were still a bit up and down in terms of results. I realised that me getting frustrated and going off my brain (as I sometimes did at training) during a match was just going to undo all the good work and upset the team bond that was still growing.

Players have to be told the truth, but there's a time and a place, a right way and a wrong way. Of course, I was still learning myself, and I reckon I was a much better coach by the end of that first A-League season.

• • •

Some bad results sent us tumbling down the table but then we beat Melbourne Victory 2 - 0 in Melbourne, cheered on by a couple of busloads of Hutch's mates from Gippsland.

• • •

First insight into housebreaking

If you'd ever wanted to burgle a house in Gippsland during John Hutchinson's playing career, you'd have done it when the Mariners played in Melbourne. Hutch was so popular in his home town the place was deserted whenever the Mariners came to Victoria.

• • •

This was the beginning of a good run. We beat the Jets 4 - 1 and for the first time there was a really strong derby atmosphere. I didnae have to duck any thrown cups of piss but there was certainly an intimidating ambience from that time on at either Hunter Stadium or Bluetongue.

We went nine games undefeated to steam into the semis and, of course, it was the Jets again. First leg in Newcastle, Matthew Osman scored with a header and Liam Reddy stomped O'Sullivan. We were furious about that and ready to smash the bastards back at home. The second leg was an official sell out (only some corporate seats were empty). Matt Thompson scored a looping goal over Vuka's head from 40 metres making it 1 - 1 on aggregate and squeaky bum time, as (the other) Fergie would say. Then Heff scored with a header in the 79th minute and we had wave after wave of Jets attacks to defend. Even Liam

Reddy was up in our box and every minute felt like an hour.

But we hung on, and Jets coach Richard Money told the media they'd been robbed. They might have dominated the last ten minutes but apart from that, they did fuck all. Money talks …

Then it was the preliminary final in Adelaide — a one legged affair. We scored early but then got battered for 83 minutes. Danny Vukovic was absolutely inspired. It was one of those days when he was simply Superman — nothing could get past him. In the heat of battle with about ten to go, I suddenly found myself laughing as Vuka clawed yet another shot out of the top corner. 'What's so funny?' asked John Crawley and I just couldn't stop laughing. 'We're gaunny win this,' I eventually said. 'Adelaide are totally smashing us but they cannae score!'

It seemed hilariously unjust given how much they dominated the game, but that's football. You've got to take your chances.

The final whistle went and we'd made the Grand Final. The inaugural A-League Grand Final against Sydney FC. We got to celebrate with the travelling fans and the beer was flowing like it really shouldnae in professional sport a week before a Grand Final, but we were all too chuffed to be too concerned with that. Mind you, some of us still managed to overdo it. The next day, Kwas threw up on the bus from the airport to Mingara where hundreds of fans were waiting for us, and the noise when we got off was unbelievable. Hundreds of Mariners fans clamouring for the team that hadnae even existed only 12 months before.

They certainly knew who we were at Mingara now, and watching the players mingle with the fans made me tremendously proud. That lack of a firewall between players and fans has always been a special part of the club culture at the Mariners. And now we'd all get to enjoy a Grand Final together.

• • •

The Grand Final media theme was predictably clichéd: Princes v Paupers; Sydney Bling v Rag-arse Rovers. I found out around this time that the Cove's name for the Mariners was the Sea Bogans. The *Telegraph* did a story showing Steve Corica in front of his Porsche, contrasted with Nigel

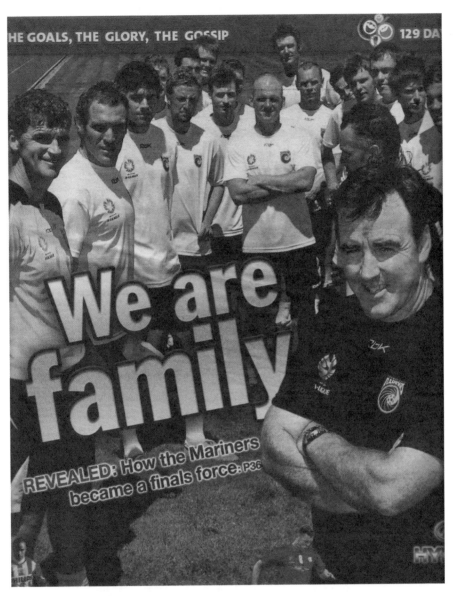

We really were a family. It was key to our success.
(*Daily Telegraph*, January 2006)

A psychic's prediction in a Tuggerah shopfront.
That's why they pay psychics the big dollars.

The predictable media theme for the Grand Final.(*Sydney Morning Herald*, March 2006)

Boogaard standing next to an old Mazda. Thing is, the Mazda wisnae Nigel's car! I'm sure they would have made a big fuss about that on *Media Watch*, but I had more important matters to deal with.

The experts gave us no chance despite the fact that we'd already beaten Sydney in Sydney that season. Mind you, for the Grand Final, a major disadvantage was playing at Allianz. It was always gaunny be full of their fans, although we did have plenty of yellow on the day — but I'll get to that.

There was an excellent buzz at training all week. The boys were relaxed because no-one expected us to trouble Bling FC and the banter was flying despite the heat and the hard work. There were cameras everywhere — unprecedented media interest in a domestic football match (although this was only shortly after the Socceroos had beaten Uruguay to make the World Cup for the first time in 32 years, so there might have been some flow on from that). Every day there were pressers and every day it seemed they got more chockers with cameras and journos — unbelievable that in just one year we'd come from the clapped out old NSL to this kind of media frenzy. It was like London in Cup Final week!

The game was on the Sunday afternoon, so on the Saturday morning we travelled down in a bus and all along the F3 there were cars with blue and gold streamers, honking like mad when they recognised us. We stayed at the Vibe at Rushcutters Bay and had a wee kick about on the park opposite on Saturday afternoon. This was about a week before the Mardi Gras and all the boys and girls were there practising their moves for their big night. We were also practising our moves — shirts off and sweaty muscles glistening in the sun — and were getting a few looks from the Mardi Gras boys, obviously wondering what float we were on.

Next day we got to the ground about an hour or so before kick off and I went out to have a look, immediately noticing the unfair allocation of yellow seats. Never mind, we'd still beat the bastards.

Back inside, the players were tense but excited. There was very little noise from outside but the dressing room had the music cranked up, the jokes were cracking and a lot of nervous energy. It was perfect.

Then the door was opened and that's when we heard the noise. We started walking up the tunnel and it sounded like Wembley, the Nou Camp and the Maracanã all piled on top of each other — absolutely deafening. (I'm getting goosebumps ten years later just thinking about it.)

There's this little patch of light up ahead as you walk down the tunnel and you feel like you're in a trance with all the noise, then you walk into light and though you thought it was loud before, that was nothing to when you're outside on the pitch and the whole stadium's packed and seething — mostly with sky blue. I snapped out of it and started shouting at the players to make sure they were all focused, but I think I'd been the worst affected. The players were fine.

We lined up 4 4 2 with Danny Vukovic in goal. There was Andrew Clark on the right with Heff on the left and a flat middle two of Wilko and Meggsy Beauchamp. In the midfield it was Wayne O'Sullivan on the right and Damien Brown on the left, with a central pair of Noel Spencer and Gumps. Up front we had Tom Pondeljak and Stuart Petrie, and on the bench were Trott, Osman, O'Grady and Kwas. I was happy enough with the side and reasonably confident of success, not least as I could tell from the players' mood that they were in the perfect place mentally.

I sat blinking in my chair, my life flashing before my eyes: Rugby Park — Box Hill — Pittwater Park — and now this! Rag-arse Rovers in the Grand Final at a sold out Sydney Football Stadium!

Mark Shield blew his whistle and we were away.

In the first five minutes we had three excellent chances, and with just a touch more composure and luck the game could have been effectively over. Gumps had an open goal to shoot at but panicked with his wrong foot and blazed wide. Petrie (co-Golden Boot winner for that season) hit a tame shot straight at Clint Bolton, and Brownie also managed to miss a shot he'd normally bury. Then Sydney started to claw their way into the contest and I remember saying after half an hour that you cannae miss that many simple chances and expect to win a football match.

That was my main message at half time. You've got to value the

The allocation of tickets was not exactly fair to the Mariners.

My coaching team at the Mariners – Alex Tobin, Ian Ferguson, John Crawley and me.

Mark Rudan and Noel Spencer — best of mates before the battle.

Always look on the bright side of life.

chances when they come along and give them the concentration and technique they deserve. But the boys were still confident. We felt we were the better team and had dominated the first half. All we had to do was go out and do the same thing, but this time take our chances.

The second half was more of an arm wrestle, a lot tighter, but as the players tired it started to open up. Anyone could have got the goal that finally mattered, but it wisnae us. Dwight Yorke had been largely contained but showed his class in the 62nd minute when he collected the ball on the right edge of the box, was closed down by three players but none of them committed to a tackle, allowing him to slip the ball to Stevie Corica who finished through Beauchamp's legs. Vuka never saw it.

'For fuck's sake!' I shouted on the bench, 'All those missed chances and then we couldnae even put a foot in!'

So, thirty to go in the GF and one nil down, but still playing the better football I thought. That was the message from the bench as we bombed forward — nothing to lose after all. But Clint Bolton was outstanding in the Sydney goal, and while we certainly dominated the last half hour we couldnae make a dent on the scoreline.

The whistle went and I felt a moment of devastating emptiness, which was immediately swamped by an incredible sense of pride for what we'd achieved. Watching Sydney FC celebrate was hard — and even harder having to hang about for all the presentations, but you've got to be gallant and respectful in defeat. It was all hugs and tears when we finally got back to the dressing room and we didnae fuck about. We were so quick onto the bus we didnae even have any beer, so I got it to stop at the Great Northern Hotel and soon the beer and banter was flowing again.

Even still, the boys weren't that keen to go back to the Leagues Club — there'd be no-one there after a loss. A police escort was waiting for us at Kariong and when we pulled up outside the club there were fifty-odd fans waiting, not too bad for a losing team hours after the game. The real surprise was when we got upstairs. There were more than five hundred and it was jumping. The players were all introduced amid absolute fucking bedlam and finally the mic was handed to me.

Deafening silence ... until some smartarse started whistling *Always look on the bright side of life*, and then it all went really berserk. Everyone joined in and the tears and laughter blended into this very intense communal joy — a feeling I've never felt before or since.

I was just so proud of what we'd achieved putting the Central Coast on the map. It wisnae just about football either and in fact I referred back to this moment — this feeling — in my first mayoral speech some years later. I really wanted people to be proud to say they came from the Central Coast and the Mariners in their first season had made a huge contribution to that.

Later, Christine and I slipped away as the team and fans continued celebrating our loss. I was totally spent but couldnae sleep. The game kept replaying in my head and I felt the steely resolve hardening — we'd lost the first Grand Final but if we got there again things would be different!

• • •

Inaugural A-League Awards Night

Stuart Petrie — Golden Boot (tied)

Lawrie McKinna — Coach of the Year

Central Coast Mariners — Most Hard Working Team

Stuart Petrie — Most Fouls Committed

• • •

A week or so afterwards, I was getting some lunch in Erina Fair when this huge bearded bloke accosted me. 'Oh fuck ... who've I pissed off now?' I wondered. But the bloke was thanking me effusively and telling me how much he loved the Mariners despite never having been into football before. 'You're so popular on the Coast right now,' he told me, 'you ought to stand for Mayor!'

I just laughed, at the time.

11

The Agony, the Ecstasy and the Agony

As we saw in Chapter 9: Thieves and Billionaires *Lawrie was offered the Sydney FC job between Seasons One and Two, but was persuaded by Singo to stay at the Mariners.*

This chapter deals with the Mariners — Years Two to Five — including winning the league but losing another Grand Final. Some amusing incidents (The Chronicles of Rag-arse Rovers) are related. There was also a first foray into the Asian Champions League, plenty of politics at CCM and, on a brief trip home to Scotland, Lawrie almost landed the Kilmarnock coaching job.

As it turned out, Bling FC were revealed to have breached the salary cap in Season One but were only punished with a three-point deduction for Season Two. Surely something else might have been heaped upon their over-privileged shoulders, like being stripped of their ACL qualification perhaps, for beating us unfairly in the Grand Final?

No, that didnae happen, and we'd have to wait another couple of years for the Mariners to qualify for Asia — but I'll get to that.

I suspect after Season One we suffered from a bit of a first season hangover. For starters there was a bit of player discontent. The boys had found out how much players at other clubs were being paid and wanted more bonus money, which the club couldnae afford. Training venues were also a problem in those days. We used 19 different training grounds in my five years in charge because there were always problems with availability, or grass coverage, or too many fuckin' goats wanting their breakfast. It was worse than playing for primary school in The Valley!

Probably my biggest problem though was player ambition. The players had realised how good they were and good players are always in demand. Heff and Meggsy Beauchamp went on loan together to FC Nurnberg and they'd both been really important in our first year. They were just about impossible to replace — not least the seven goals Heff scored from left back! We did get Tony Vidmar though and he was quality — as you'd expect from an ex-Rangers legend.

There were also eight local players in the squad by then: Brad Porter, Jamie McMaster, Damien Brown, Andrew Clark, James Holland, Ollie Bozanic, Matthew Trott and Matt Simon. The crowd loved the locals and Season Two seemed to start brightly enough. We made the final of the pre-season cup, losing on penalties to Adelaide, but in the league we won only one of our first seven matches and never really got out of the blocks.

We finished sixth but the biggest win was Christine and I becoming Aussie citizens mid-pitch before the last game of the season — one of the proudest days of my life. The game had been held up by bushfires, which is strangely apt, like nature's way of saying: Are you sure you want this? But there were thousands of people all cheering us in the stands so how could we not want part of that? It was truly humbling and very memorable (even if the whole second season wisnae).

When the third season rolled around I could feel the difference early. The squad had changed a bit — Petrie, Spencer and O'Sullivan had all retired and in came Andrew Redmayne and Saso Petrovski. I made Wilko captain and that year saw the emergence of Mile Jedinak as a seriously dominant player at A-League level. Heff was back, playing brilliantly until he broke his leg on the day of his brother's wedding, and Nicky Mrdja was finally free of injury. He played so well in fact that he was picked for the Socceroos, but then broke down again and that was the end of him. Such a shame because he was that rarest of commodities — an outstandingly good Australian striker. We just don't make them in this country (like we make goalkeepers and defenders) and I reckon if he'd not had his long term injuries we may have seen someone approaching Viduka-like quality. He really was that good.

And speaking of famous Socceroos — at the start of the year Singo rang up and said: 'Do you want John Aloisi? I hear he's available.'

Of course I did, so I rang his agent — Paddy Dominguez — who told me that, yes, John was available ... for $800k per season.

I rang Singo back, who said: 'Who the fuck does he think he is, wanting eight hundred grand to play fuckin' football?' So that idea was binned — for a while.

The season kicked off with a 1 - 0 win at Sydney FC scored by Saso — it was great result to get anything at Sydney and it really set us up for the year. For a football team there's nothing like momentum to breed confidence. We beat Wellington 3 - 0 at home, then against Queensland Roar (as they still were) Kwas scored the winner from a training ground set piece. Best of all, every other game in the first three

Becoming citizens, the best moment of a disappointing second season.

rounds had been drawn so we were six points clear before the fourth round!

Suddenly we were full of confidence and swagger — important players were getting goals. We got beaten 2 - 1 after Viddie got sent off against Adelaide, but Saso kept banging 'em in. A crucial game was away at Wellington when he scored in the 91st minute. Then there was an amazing game against Sydney FC when Hutch hit two screamers into the top corners, but we couldnae get the third for a win.

At home against ten man Melbourne Victory we were 1 - 0 down deep in the second half when there were two more red cards (one each). Somehow amid all the chaos and carnage we managed a couple of goals to Sasho (83rd) and Tom Pondeljak (88th) to win 2 - 1, yet another brilliant win that spoke volumes about the team's character and toughness.

Of course, football being what it is, injuries happen and momentum slows. John Aloisi was still clubless and now willing to play for far less than the start of the year. Mind you, the club still couldnae afford him so I rang Singo and told him the relevant numbers.

'Done,' said Singo, 'Get him!'

Those readers who've paid attention might remember my old team mate from Kilmarnock — Coby. The lad that welcomed me to pre-season training with the cock-tying initiation ceremony. Well, he was coming out to Australia for a visit and that was about the time we signed Aloisi.

The local radio (2GO) ran a competition for a number of people to come to my house for a barbeque to meet Johnny. There were kids everywhere and jumping castles and caterers all over my front yard. They're all waiting for Johnny when a limo pulls up in the driveway. The TV cameras, journalists and kids all surround the limo going mad with excitement, when Coby gets out with his bags from Scotland and says: 'All this for me? Thanks Lawrie, I'm deeply touched.'

Johnny played 15 games and scored seven goals for us — a great bit of business. But more than that he was a fantastic signing who brought some real cachet to the team and was such a lovely bloke. The boys loved having him.

Mind you, we were no longer top of the table when we played an absolute classic of a match at home to Sydney FC. The 22nd of December 2007 will long be remembered by fans of the two clubs, although far more fondly by the Sky Blues. We were two up early after goals to Jedi and Aloisi, but then Vuka copped a red card for one of his kamikaze runs outside the box (where he handled the ball) and that totally changed the game. They were back on terms by the 50th minute, but then we went ahead again through Greg Owens. But Biddle and Santalab scored for Sydney and we were one down with only minutes to play. It was an interesting afternoon for Kwas who scored the equaliser in the 86th minute, only to be sent off in the 4th minute of added time for a handball on the line. Ufuk Talay put away the penalty for the last kick of the game, which would have been fantastic for Sydney, excellent television for the neutrals and heartbreaking for us.

It got worse on New Year's Eve when we were smashed at home in front of 18,000 fans: 5 - 2. Then two weeks later we were beaten in front of 19,000 by the Jets. The wheels were wobbling and in danger of falling off but going into the last round we were third and still a mathematical chance if results went our way.

We had to play Wellington and win by at least two to have any chance at all. Going into added time we only led by one. Then, in the 94th minute, in driving rain, Tommy Pondeljak desperately chased a ball to the byeline and cut it back to the edge of the box where Kwas sidefooted into the top corner. I turned to Fergie on the bench and said: 'That's just won us the league.'

The next day was Sydney v Melbourne Victory in Sydney. Now Sydney needed to win by two goals to go top so I rang Kevin Muscat to ask him to do his best. 'Don't worry,' he said. 'We don't like Sydney so we won't let them beat us.'

I was happy with that until I saw Melbourne had changed their keeper (a very young Mitch Langerak making his starting debut) when they'd nothing left to play for. I was cursing Ernie Merrick when Stevie Corica scored in the third minute, with the young keeper very much at fault. But Muskie was as good as his word. It finished 2 - 2 and as I paced my living room like a caged lion, I was impressed to see him throw his body on the line in the last minute to prevent Santalab.

Just one game to go and again a team needed to win by two goals to take the league. Roar went to Adelaide in excellent form and with Adelaide having had a miserable year. Danny Tiatto got himself sent off just before half time and suddenly the text messages were flying around the Mariners boys. We all made our way to Terrigal Pub to watch the second half and as news of our presence got about the place filled with fans coming to celebrate with us. Roar had to make up a four goal deficit and as the seconds ticked away and they made no dent on the scoreboard, the joy began to bubble over. Lyall Gorman slapped $1000 on the bar and the party kicked off.

We'd won the fucking league! Rag-arse Rovers from Gosford had beaten Australia's best over the home and away season! It's what you really play for — to be top of the league when all the dust settles. Grand Finals are exhilarating but they come down to the toss of a coin. Coaches get true satisfaction from excellence and consistency — which is what you need to be number one after the final round.

The first semi was against the Jets in Newcastle and we were fucking well robbed. Johnny Aloisi's perfectly legal goal was disallowed and then the Griffiths brothers (Adam and Joel) both scored to put them very much in the box seat to make the Grand Final. Joel Griffiths (known as Sackwhacker to the fans for the time he punched a linesman in the scrotum at Bluetongue) was a special player who for mysterious reasons never quite received the recognition he probably deserved — certainly not in the national team — but he was the scourge of the Mariners for a number of seasons.

In the return leg in front of a sold out Bluetongue Stadium, my message to the players was simple: we just want to score one goal. Let's concentrate on that — one goal. (We'd worry about the others later.) Kwas, who had a habit of scoring important goals, scored with a deflected shot in the first half and 19,000 erupted in ecstasy.

'Don't panic!' I was shouting at half time. 'They're rattled ... just keep up the pressure and be patient. The goals will take care of themselves.'

Sure enough, Saso scored in the 74th minute and the tie was even — and that's how it finished. That meant extra time, with the prospect of penalties afterwards, but in the 96th minute Saso scored again with one of the greatest goals I've ever seen — smashed in from the corner of the box. The response from the crowd was probably the best atmosphere I've ever experienced at Bluetongue. Huge! Nineteen thousand roaring and urging the team to the finish. The poor old Jets fans couldnae believe what was happening. They'd let slip a two goal lead, but I say it was karma for Aloisi's goal being wrongly chalked off in the first leg!

So, once again we'd made the Grand Final, with the right to play at home. But the FFA adjudged Bluetongue too small for a game of such importance and, despite our furious protests, scheduled the game for Allianz. It was just as well Sydney had already been knocked out by the Roar or we'd have been livid (as well as furious). Again we were playing the Jets after they beat Roar 3 - 2 in the preliminary final.

• • •

So what was different this time after losing in Season One?

Thousands of fans turned up for a waterfront farewell, which was hair on the back of the neck stuff. My parents also had come out from Scotland to experience the massive occasion and I was so proud to see so many thousands of Mariners fans before we left, on the road, and at the stadium.

The team had more or less picked itself all year but for this match I had to think hard about my two most creative players. Pondeljak had been injured and Gumps was out of sorts — in the end, I started them both on the bench.

The game itself though, for all the excitement, was pretty dour. The Jets went to 3 5 2 — which really surprised but didnae trouble us. We dominated all the stats that mattered, but in the 64th minute, Viddie stumbled on the ball, Bridge bolted away with it and bent it around Vuka (his best mate). Then for 25 minutes we absolutely pumped them without creating any clear cut chances.

Then the moment of destiny — time added on — 94th minute. We had a corner and all our players were in the box, including Vuka. The ball was swung over, James Holland protecting the near post jumped up and every person in the ground saw him punch the ball away.

Close to my proudest moment in football.

Except the ref.

Mark Shields was adamant and Vuka (rather unwisely) slapped his admonishing hand, leading to a red card that was to cost Danny dearly. We didnae get a crack at extra time and the way momentum had swung we'd surely have won it. I didnae realise Danny had been sent off for striking the ref until later at the press conference and all the media were trying to wind me up, but I wouldnae criticise Shields over the blatant handball. If he didnae see it he couldnae give it. End of.

But my week from hell wisnae over. The following day was an FFA season review meeting. In the late afternoon, an FFA media guy says to me: 'There's a problem with your boys' Mad Monday.'

'What's the problem?' I asked.

'Apparently Andre Gumprecht has come dressed as Adolf Hitler.'

'So?'

'Well, it's disrespectful to Jews,' he hissed, looking furtively over his shoulder. 'The Chairman is Jewish.'

I said: 'Do you understand what Mad Monday is about? You're supposed to dress as somehow relevant to your culture or background. Gumps is German ... he's come dressed as someone who *wished* he was German! It's a joke, for fuck's sake!'

But there's no sense of humour in this stupid world sometimes. Everyone's so fuckin' serious about shite that doesnae matter, and on top of the loss, and Danny's suspension it was close to my worst week in football.

Still, we had won the league and had an Asian Champions League campaign to look forward to.

One other positive postscript to all that, some months later Mark Shields apologised out of the blue. He came up from Sydney and had lunch with me, and deeply expressed his regret at not having seen the handball (which would have changed everything). Certainly made me feel a bit better about the whole sorry episode, as I'd always liked Mark as a ref and respected the gesture, not least as he came all the way up from Sydney to apologise face to face.

119

The Chronicles of Rag-arse Rovers

During Lawrie's time as coach at the Mariners there were any number of incidents which subtly (or not so subtly) underscored the financial gulf that separated the Mariners from other clubs. For starters they never had a long-term dedicated training ground — 19 different grounds were used by Lawrie, most of them just ordinary council grounds open to the public. The following incidents give some idea of what life was like at Rag-arse Rovers.

One of the grounds we used for a while was Jubilee Oval at The Entrance. We're training there one day and playing a fairly intense eight-vs-eight game, when a woman walking her dog proceeds blithely through the middle of us. I opened my mouth to tell the boys to watch out for her, and to my utter disbelief the dog stops and drops a steaming great shite in the centre of our pitch.

'What the fuck do you think you're doing?' I asked her. She completely ignored me and continued on her way, perfectly calm with her unburdened pooch trotting at her side. It was unbelievable arrogance, and of course Muggins has to remove the shite with a plastic training cone while the boys are collapsed in fits of laughter.

After that we had to do a shite check before every session. Can you imagine Sir Alex Ferguson or Arsene Wenger having to do a shite check before training? Mesut Ozil could be complaining about turd all over his boots and Wenger would just shrug and say he did not see it.

Another memorable incident was Johnny Aloisi's first ever training session. We're talking about one of the greatest Socceroos to grace the EPL, Serie A and La Liga (still the only Australian to have played in all three of those leagues) and, of course, the scorer of that penalty on 16th of November 2005. There were few bigger players in the Australian game at the time and for us to land his signature for a guest stint was just huge.

Anyway, he turns up for his first ever session with his new A-League club, and there in the middle of the training ground is a burnt out car.

We're talking about a player who's been carefully managed and nurtured his whole professional life. Nothing was ever too much for someone who'd graced sides like Cremonese, Coventry City and Osasuna. Well, sorry Johnny but a training pitch without burnt out cars was too much to expect at Rag-arse Rovers. Welcome to the team!

Another time we were training on a cricket pitch with no ground markings, so Alex Tobin and I had to pace out the sides of the ground — 100 paces long by 70 wide. Well, he's clearly got longer legs than me because after a few minutes of playing we realised the pitch was totally askew. It wisnae a rectangle, it was a fuckin' rhombus. Only at Rag-arse Rovers.

John Hutchinson continues the theme …

Rag-arse Rovers? That's being kind! We used to meet at Body Fuel Terrigal with two vans and all the players waiting for a message to see where Lawrie could find a ground so we could train. From hockey fields to schools to cricket ovals or even a little drive down to Sydney! We knew the fruit and the lunch would be there as Lawrie would get that on his way to training, but if we had goalposts that was a bonus. Otherwise we'd use poles or jumpers as goals. No bibs? That's okay because we could play skins v shirts.

Another time, playing Newcastle away first game of the season, we didn't even know if the strips would be there but they got delivered to the stadium just as we were coming in from the warm up! These days I play All Age Threes for Terrigal and if I can be confident of one thing, it is that the strip will always be there and ready to wear. But at Rag-arse Rovers, it was always touch and go.

• • •

Weird Science: Asian Champions League

More than ten years into membership of the Asian Confederation, Australian teams (and fans) still have a funny relationship with Asia — not least the Champions League, which has never really fired the fans' imagination. (With the possible exception of RBB towards the end of the Wanderers' successful campaign).

Not so the players. The players love the opportunity to visit other countries and play football in some super-modern stadiums — often with massive, passionate crowds. It's hugely exciting, for a young player in particular, to get out of Australia and be centre of attention in a vast exotic city.

Less exciting for the clubs themselves though ...

We couldnae afford it.

We got a fantastic draw against Tianjin Teda, Pohang Steelers and Kawasaki Frontale, but the club couldnae afford to go and it really was touch and go as to whether we could actually take part. There was only so much money in the travelling budget, but fortunately Alex Wilkinson's dad, Rob, was a travel agent and he did a brilliant job of finding us the best deals. Mind you, the best deal was Cathay, which meant we always had to fly via Hong Kong. The boys might have found such indirect flying intensely irritating if Andrew Clark hadnae told them it was being done deliberately for sports science reasons. That's why I love footballers: if you say it with a straight face they'll believe any load of shite you tell them.

Our first game in the ACL was at home against the South Korean Pohang Steelers — the eventual winners of the tournament. We did very well to come away from that with a 0 - 0 draw, so went to Tianjin a week later with a bit of confidence.

It's an interesting town, Tianjin, newly industrialised and very modern. The stadium is a beautiful, purpose built ground with a playing surface like a perfect green carpet and stands built right on top of you like the Anfield Kop — very intimidating when full and we already knew the game was a 27,000 seat sell-out. It certainly got the boys fired up, training on that pitch, and even Pete Turnbull and Lyall Gorman were inspired to get kitted up and kick a ball about!

Quite a few of our fans also had come along for the historic occasion and, like the team, they were treated very courteously by our Chinese hosts. Until the team forgot to read the script and went 2 - 1 up with not long to go. The courtesy was replaced with flying bottles and angry booing. They were chucking bottles at us on the bench also and from point blank! But the inability of the fans to hit a big

Scottish bastard from ten feet with a bottle was pretty much reflective of their team's ability to hit the target. They did manage a late equaliser, unfortunately, and the field was totally covered in bottles by furious fans who'd expected to win easily.

So, two draws to start the campaign against two excellent teams. We could have won both of those games so there was reason to be confident we might get out of the group phase.

Then the reality check. Nine and a half thousand turned up at home to see us play Kawasaki Frontale. After Nick Mrdja missed two one-on-ones in the first five minutes we were never in it. We were gubbed 5 - 0 by possibly the best team I've ever played against. Their passing, touch and movement were different class and, to make things worse, we next had to go and play them in Japan (via Hong Kong of course — sports science and all that).

The boys were happy, at least, in Kawasaki. The facilities were brilliant and we spent a lot of time on defensive shape. But then it rained for 24 hours before the game and my heart sank as I thought of the way the ball would zip around on that surface. A team with their pace and movement would tear us apart on a slick pitch, but to my great surprise and gratification we played superbly well and were still 0 - 0 at half time. Then they scored straight after the restart but Matty Simon hit back immediately and we had several chances to win it.

• • •

Sixth insight into coaching

Never make a change when about to defend a corner.

Not even if your goalkeeper is lying unconscious in a pool of blood — you just don't do it when defending a corner.

Never.

• • •

They had a corner in the 81st minute and I'd been wanting to make a sub, but you just don't do it when defending a corner. It's one of those fundamental life skills like: not drinking bleach or not sticking your finger down a funnelweb hole. You'd have to be fuckin' mad.

Anyway, I made the change and they scored from the corner.

Later in the dressing room (after breaking my toe on the door) I stupidly had a go at Heff for leaving his man. Then he had a go at me and the next thing we're both being restrained from killing each other. Five minutes later we were both hugging and crying and best of mates again, and as we left the stadium to get back on the bus I was gobsmacked to see 30-odd Mariners fans standing in the rain still clapping and cheering for us. Certainly put things back in perspective.

Our next away trip was the return leg in Pohang — a really fascinating place and home of the fastest download speed in the world. I've always had a tradition that, when travelling, the team should go for a walk to soak up a bit of the local atmos, but on this occasion for some reason the boys had all gone missing. When I finally tracked them down they were all holed up in (I won't say whose) room watching midget porn, which is a thing in South Korea.

Another thing was couples in matching outfits. Everywhere you looked you'd see men and women wearing the same clothes and holding hands like a mini-team. I could just imagine what Christine would say if she caught me dressing up in her clothes!

The game was very open and, after being 1 - 0 down at half time, Kwas put us ahead 2 - 1 and I started to think that just maybe we could do something in the group. But the true difference between the big Asian teams and A-League teams was money, and therefore the quality of strikers they could afford. Pohang had a Brazilian up front by the name of Denilson, who got two late goals, completing his hat trick and putting qualification beyond us.

So it was a dead rubber when Tianjin came to Gosford for the last game, but that didn't stop them from playing like a pack of pork chops. It was an absolute disgrace the way the Chinese would fall to the ground and roll about shrieking at every opportunity. Even worse was the inability of the officials to cope with it. After going 1 - 0 up the Tianjin players just stopped the game by pretending to be injured every 30 seconds or so — it was impossible to play against and the stands were loud with booing.

It was a huge relief when the ACL was over. We'd started with two points, and that's how we finished, but we learned a thing or two about how hard it is to compete in Asia. It absolutely puts the later achievements of Adelaide United (finalists) and Western Sydney (champions) into perspective. Those were wonderful performances that said a great deal about the Australian ability to compete regardless of the conditions and the financial numbers stacked against us.

As for the A-League that year, we finished fourth in a largely forgettable season. Danny was suspended for a ridiculous five months which meant he missed the Olympics.

Peter Turnbull said to me: 'Are you interested in Bozza?'

Mark Bosnich?

Seriously?

The same Mark Bosnich who'd had all those well publicised problems in the UK. Did I really want to bring that sort of character into our dressing room with its famous 'No Dickheads' policy?

Almost against my better judgment I had a few chats with him over the phone from London, and I have to admit it was his enthusiasm that sold me. Obviously, I knew he was a great keeper, but he was getting on a bit and didn't look that fit in the recent footage I'd seen of him working with Ed de Goey to get back in shape. Plus he was Bozza, with all the baggage that comes with being Bozza. But his football intelligence and enthusiasm, as I judged it over the phone, made him irresistible.

He was absolutely brilliant as it turned out. The minute he walked into our dressing room he was one of the boys and extremely popular. The only issue he had was his diva performance on learning there was no hair dryer in the rooms. Seriously, you'd think anyone who'd played under Sir Alex would see that as a massive bonus, but not our Bozza. Very concerned about his coiffure that young man.

He didn't train that hard either.

And wasn't much interested in a pre-game warm-up.

Mark Bosnich – the only man ever to receive a standing ovation from both
Sydney FC and Mariners fans. (Photo courtesy Cam Wheeler Photography)

'What's his fuckin' caper?' I asked John Crawley as Bozza did absolutely fuck all before a pre-season game against Sydney FC.

'Don't worry,' said JC, 'he knows his body … he's a professional.'

And in all honesty, he was outstanding in that game — saved a penalty and made a couple of other world class saves. I substituted him just before the end and he got a standing ovation from both sets of fans — which disnae happen often in Australian football. We had him for two months and he was just fantastic for the club, and I do take some satisfaction for being part of his redemption as a sports personality. He was a class act, though.

One other satisfying aspect of that year was our resilience. Twice we came back from 3 - 0 down, first at Adelaide and then three weeks later at Sydney. It really demonstrated the fighting spirit we'd created, but that was the year we let Mile Jedinak go and chase his dreams in Europe. I'd never realised before how one player can so fundamentally change a team. We never recovered from his loss, but I'll deal with that in another chapter.

We limped into the finals that year and were quickly bundled out by Brisbane, but straight after the game Christine called me over to the fence, upset because one of our grandkids had just been taken to hospital. As I was talking to her someone from within the nearby Mariners fans yelled out: 'Lawrie McKinna, you're a cunt!'

'Who the fuck said that?' I shouted back in anger, and walked over to them with Christine trying to drag me back. I asked again, furious — not least as I knew that this group of fans were the ones to whom I'd given all the spare players' tickets.

None of them said a word. After I'd stormed off Christine gave them a total bollocking, as only she can — especially the bloke who said it. Yes, she saw him, the cowardly piece of shit.

Next day at the airport to head home, one of the Coast FM blokes (who had been calling for my head on the radio) sauntered over all friendly, so I said to him: 'This is nice … so you don't want me sacked after all?'

He just mumbled something and walked away, but that was the

beginning of the anti-Lawrie campaign that plagued me throughout the following season.

• • •

The less said about my fifth season at CCM the better.

My entire career had always been built on great relationships with players, fans and media. You don't have to have great relationships with administrators — we're all just professionals doing a job and we get on with it irrespective of personalities. But personality is crucial as far as players, fans and media are concerned. These are the people passionate about football so you've got to get along with them. That had never been a problem for me but it certainly became one in season five.

We actually started fairly well but hit the skids in December and went nine games without a win. At such times you start to doubt yourself so I got Tom Sermani in to have a look at us. He said everything looked pretty good — we'd just been unlucky. But the season was running out.

There were constant issues with training grounds and the cash-strapped club cutting corners every chance they could. The players had had enough and everyone was getting on each other's tits with me in the middle trying to hold it all together.

One day near the end of the season we were training at Ourimbah with no equipment. Kwas had a shot and missed and Peter Turnbull standing by said: "You couldn't hit the side of a barn!'

'How do you know I missed when we don't have any fuckin' goalposts?' replied Kwas, and I had to step in to defuse a nasty situation. I think I knew in my water that day that it was all turning to shite.

There was a year left on my contract but everyone and everything has a use-by date. Lyall contacted Arnie to sound him out about taking over. I was a tad pissed off it started behind my back, but I also knew it was time for a change — not just for me but also the players, and even the fans. The Alex Fergusons and Arsene Wengers of this world are incredibly rare and five years in the A-League with one club is an absolute marathon.

Lyall and I started meeting with Arnie to talk about what our new roles might be. I was kicked upstairs to be General Manager of Football and, while I was very happy with the arrangement, it did strike me as ironic that it was now my job to provide for Arnie all the facilities and players that had been refused to me.

There's no denying that it worked though. The Mariners had an excellent few years under Arnie with me still in place as General Manager of Football and then just as club ambassador. But life moves on and I was soon to have other fish to fry — Chinese ones.

• • •

One funny little postscript to the 2010 season ...

On our way to the World Cup in South Africa, Christine and I went home for two weeks to The Valley for my parents' Golden Wedding anniversary. I read in the paper that the Killie job had just been offered to Steve Kean but he'd knocked it back to take over at Blackburn. So I phoned Jimmy Clarke (who'd been captain when I was last playing) and his wife Anne answered the phone. She worked in the back office and told me the job was still available.

She put me through to the chairman's secretary and the next thing I knew I was talking to Michael Johnston in the Park Hotel at Rugby Park about what was happening in Kilmarnock, going through my career, outlining my ideas for getting the best out of an under-resourced group of footballers and how to engage a football community. The meeting went very well and was followed by another the next Monday with Michael and two other board members. Again the meeting went really well — so well in fact that I told Christine to start looking for houses.

The chairman asked me to meet him at the training venue at Glasgow University, but before that I met with an old mate, John McGarry, a *News of the World* journalist who was waiting for a scoop. My first premonition that maybe something was wrong happened when the chairman rang to say he'd been delayed so the head groundsman would show me around instead. I was shown the facilities, which were very good, but I was adamant that Killie should be training in Kilmarnock (despite the fact that most of the players lived in Glasgow).

Maybe I'd been too adamant because the next thing I heard, Mixu Paatelainen had the job. I cannae really complain as Mixu did fairly well, so a good decision by the Kilmarnock board. I was disappointed though as it would have been the perfect homecoming. It would also have been nice to have bought the house in Darvel across the road from Christine's dad. But no matter how successful I might have been in Scotland, we'd always have returned to Australia.

12

The Extra Mile

During his years coaching Northern Spirit and the Mariners (and also while General Manager of Football), Lawrie signed an impressive list of players who went on to play for the Socceroos and/or have successful careers overseas. Lawrie's Socceroos include: Mat Ryan, Mark Milligan, Bernie Ibini, James Holland, Trent Sainsbury, Michael Beauchamp, Alex Wilkinson, Matt Simon, Ollie Bozanic and, of course, Mile Jedinak — the Socceroos and Crystal Palace captain. There was also John Hutchinson who became a Maltese international, and others he signed include: Mustafa Amini, Danny Vukovic, Michael McGlinchey, Nick Mrdja. These players are household names today and all have one thing in common — they were given a chance in professional football by Lawrie who must have the best Socceroo conversion rate of any A-League coach.

I've said from the start that I never really had a huge amount of footballing talent myself. I was big, fast and strong in the air but that's about it. Still, I managed to make the best of what I had which enabled me to compete with far more gifted players. And while I may not have shared their gifts I certainly knew a gift for football when I saw it.

So what do I look for when assessing the potential of a lad for professional football? It's not rocket science, any young lad who is reasonably athletic can be turned into a footballer. But there are three aspects I always look for to take a player to the next level: attitude, work rate and ability, with ability the least important because players with ability are a dime a dozen — and I'd never be even looking at someone without good basic technique.

Attitude. This is simply about being a good person and able to fit into a team. The Mariners have a famous 'No Dickheads' policy which has been very much the key to their success in the first decade of the A-League. I had the same policy at Northern Spirit and it meant that the only lads I signed were happy to get along with the other blokes and be part of a team's delicate balance. Just one arsehole can destroy everything you've built. Every new personality coming into the squad has to be assessed not only on their own merit, but on how well they'll blend with the personalities already in place. I've no time for prima donnas and I've weeded out a few in my time. Some of them had stacks of ability but they never made the grade because, frankly, they were dickheads.*

Work rate. It doesnae matter how good you are if you're not prepared to put in a shift for the team. My teams were never good enough to carry passengers so I've only ever picked lads who would work until they dropped, and then get up and go again. Refusal to do so was a sign of poor attitude and I've had to be fairly blunt on occasion with young players who assumed they were already fit enough. You're never fit enough to play in my teams.

Ability. Last of all is ability. I've always looked for boys who could do the simple things well and get the easy things right most of the time (like Alex Wilkinson or Nick Montgomery). I'd build my team around reliable players who never made mistakes and then throw in two or three with that little spark of something extra that can change a game.

So what is that 'something extra'? We all know it when we see it — the dash of flair that doesnae always come off but, when it does, results in something truly memorable.

Football, especially professional football, is a game of really tight margins — goals are hard to get and just one decides a game. Professional coaches know their own teams like the back of their hand and study the other teams obsessively. Strengths and weaknesses are assessed and analysed for hours by the coaching staff and senior players and strategies worked out to make the best of our strengths while exploiting the enemy's weakness — if any. Games really are like chess matches at this level so players have to be incredibly disciplined to carry

---

* The deluxe version of this book has a list of all the dickheads I've encountered in football, but if you're reading this footnote you must have bought the cheaper version.

out the coach's instructions. If they willnae do that, then they won't get picked the following week.

In this sort of environment — with every player going like clockwork — it's the special player with the unusual talent that can make a difference. Mind you, he can also lose you the game if he stuffs up so he has to have the courage to try something that may get him a bollocking if it doesnae work. Some of these special abilities are obvious — pace for example. Pace is so important in modern football because the game's all about creating time on the ball — time to do something with the ball. Pace buys you extra time and takes it away from the enemy.

Another obvious talent is shooting from distance. Mile Jedinak was brilliant at that and could change a result with a 25 metre shot — dead ball or open play. He's done it for the Socceroos, for Crystal Palace, and plenty of times for the Mariners.

Other special abilities are less obvious, quick feet for example, which is different from pace. If a player can take three steps to your two, he'll beat you every time because he's got the extra touch that you won't be able to respond to. Lionel Messi and Cristiano Ronaldo are blessed with incredibly quick feet even though neither (Messi in particular) have blistering pace — they still leave defenders clutching at straws because of their sleight of foot.

I've not seen a lot of players in my time with that sort of ability, although Tommy Pondeljak was a special player. At the Mariners there was Michael McGlinchey, Tommy Rogic and Bernie Ibini (although Tommy was Arnie's signing) who could usually beat the first man. Beating a man, anywhere on the park, immediately puts the team in an advantageous position, but if you couldn't do that most of the time, you didnae have permission to try.

A more common type of special ability is vision. Players like Mustafa Amini are all about what they see and can make happen with a tricky pass into the path of a player the defence haven't picked up. I first heard of Amini when he was just 16 and playing with the Australian Institute of Sport. There'd been a few whispers about this frizzy-haired wunderkind down in Canberra so I was a very interested observer one day when the Mariners Youth Team had a game against the AIS at Seymour Shaw Oval. We had four first team players in the squad that day and they never got a kick! Musti just took the piss for the whole 90 minutes as my jaw hung lower and lower.

The thing about Musti was that he wasn't just about the tricks and beating a man, the real talent was his incredible vision, which is something the kids don't usually develop until their twenties. Musti had a really advanced ability to see everything happening around him and play the right ball to the right player at exactly the right time.

The coach of the AIS back then was Gary Van Egmond and I asked him if was this a regular performance or something out of the box. 'No, he's always like that,' said Gary. 'The boy's got a chance to make it.'

'More than a chance,' I thought, and I signed him within a week. He did brilliantly for the Mariners and has since been learning his trade in Europe. He's still only young but has the ability to go a very long way.

One of the players I most enjoy talking about is Matt Simon, probably because he's the one who most reminds me of myself as a player. Back in the first season at the Mariners Matty was an apprentice plasterer who was always plaguing me on the phone for a trial. I'd seen him play in the local premier league Grand Final in 2004 and knew he'd been the league's top scorer, but it's a big jump from local league to A-League. Eventually I caved in and let him come along to training and, sure enough, he wisnae so effective against professional players. 'What do you think?' I asked my assistant Ian Ferguson as we watched him running about like a maniac in an eight-vs-eight trial.

'Like fuckin' Bambi on ice,' was Ian's assessment of the gangling, awkward youngster. But there was something about him I liked. He didnae have the best first touch, but he was big, fast and absolutely unrelenting in his desire to cause problems for defenders and goalkeepers. Right from the start I could see that defenders hated playing against him — even if they usually had his measure, at first. He must've trained with us for several months before I signed him as a short term injury replacement, which eventually turned into a full season (and was later extended for several seasons).

Being a local lad, from East Gosford, he was popular with the

Matt Simon, unconventional but highly effective.

John Hutchinson was always a favourite with the fans —
but check out the grinning berk in the background in an Arsenal T-shirt!

Top: Musti just seemed to float across the turf sometimes.

Above: Oliver Bozanic, a very cultured player but learned to shoot at Avoca FC, so Iain Fyfe couldnae be arsed tackling him.

Left: I worried I was compromising my No Dickheads policy to sign Trent Sainsbury but I was wrong. Lovely bloke and excellent player.

fans, but they had to be patient with him. He didn't score at all in his first year, but he was effective. He made a difference to the team and that was recognised with a call up to the Olyroos squad as a stand by player for a pre-Olympic tournament. Sure enough, at the last minute he was called into the squad and ended up getting four goals in the tournament. When he came back to Australia he was full of confidence and, the very day of his return, I sat him on the bench for our opening game of the season away to Newcastle. With ten to go we were one nil down so I threw him on — jetlag and all — and he got us the equaliser, his first goal for the Mariners after about 19 games!

From that time he never looked back, adding better touch and brains to his natural speed and aggression. He wound up playing two games for Holger Osieck's Socceroos and still holds the Mariners' all time goal scoring record. After a very dodgy beginning, he's arguably the Mariners fans' favourite ever player (either him or Hutch).

There are plenty of others I like talking about, players who got their first pro contract with me and went on to do something special. Mark Milligan, for example, just showed up at Northern Spirit training as a cheeky 17-year-old wanting a trial. Impressed by his gall I let him train and saw straight away what a tidy player he was. I said to Gary McGuinness* the Spirit Youth Team coach: 'I want you to sign him on a youth contract.'

'I've not got any places left,' he said. I thought, 'Fuck it! He's too good to miss,' and signed him on a full professional contract (such as we had in those days).

The very next week he started against Sydney Olympic and gave away a penalty in a 1 - 0 loss. But he still had an excellent game and has gone on to show what a valuable player he is. You can play him anywhere and he'll always do a job — as he did for the Socceroos during the Asian Cup and for Melbourne Victory in the 2015 Grand Final. I'd even say he's gone to a whole new level in recent times and wouldnae look out of place in a much bigger league.

Two of Mark's current Socceroo team mates are Trent Sainsbury and Alex Wilkinson. Wilko's excellent, but Sainsbury's different class. I heard

---

* With whom I'd played for Dundee United in that trial against Brechin.

about him from his agent, Tony Rallis, who never talked about anything else at the time. Everything was Trent this ... Sainsbury that ... so I had a look at him and immediately saw what Tony was on about.

But when he came in to talk terms he clearly had a bit of an attitude — didnae half fancy himself — so I was deeply concerned about the integrity of my 'No Dickheads' policy. I was also keenly aware that Melbourne Heart wanted him so I had a decision to make. Fortunately, my first impression of young Trent was quite wrong. It was just a bit of youthful bravado and he turned out to be a lovely young bloke who absolutely flourished alongside Wilko and Patrick Zwaanswijk when given his chance by Arnie. He's got an excellent football brain, can play a long pass with devastating effect (such as his ball to set up Luongo's goal in the Asian Cup Final) and is super fast by defender standards. Fast enough to fix his mistakes and even the mistakes of his team mates.

After playing in the Eredivisie he's now making a fortune in China and is one of the first picked for the Socceroos. I would not be remotely surprised if young Trent captains his country at some stage.

As for Wilko, I've been calling for his selection in the Socceroos for donkey's years and I'm overjoyed that he's finally made it. Selection was long overdue but Wilko's problem was that he was one of those players who does their job so calmly and efficiently that he never gets noticed — invisible except to his team mates and a few good judges.

I first had him at Spirit and immediately described him as 'Mr Eight-out-of-Ten'. From his earliest days he was the perfect professional, always putting in an eight-out-of ten performance. Always had a very sound head on his shoulders also — he trialled with Rangers at the age of 18, and then knocked back their offer when he decided they weren't the right club for him! As a lifelong Rangers fanatic, that was hard for me to take, but the Blue Sea of Ibrox's loss was the Mariners' gain.

He was one of the very first I signed when I became Mariners' coach and shortly after made him captain — at the ripe old age of 23. Wilko was always mature beyond his years though and he turned out to be a perfect choice — a quiet man who leads by example and continues to put in eight out of ten performances for the Socceroos. He was also recently picked in the 2014-15 K-League team of the

Mister 'Eight out of Ten' collects his just reward.

season. That's a tough, demanding competition so it just goes to show I'm not the only one who rates him.

Another of my international players was John Hutchinson. Hutcho never played for the Socceroos, but he did manage a couple of games for Malta so that qualifies him for this very exclusive chapter of my book. Hutcho was another I had from the bad old days at Spirit when there wisnae enough money to pay for the ground hire, let alone luxuries like food and rent. Hutch was actually a bit of a dickhead when I met him, way too laid back and a bit of a Joe Cool type personality, so I quickly had to tell him: pull your head in or you're out the door pal.

First game in 2002 against Brisbane Strikers (coached by Kossie) Hutch got the ball in front of our bench, dragged it inside onto his left foot, then back onto his right and slammed it into the top right corner from 30 yards. I remember hugging him after the game and he's been a hugger ever since and a really important part of the dressing room.

When I was first appointed coach of the Mariners he was just about to give the game away as there was no future in football for a young man trying to make a career. I brought him up to Gosford and showed him the stadium — the training facilities at Mingara — and football suddenly seemed like a viable proposition. So Hutch signed and the fantastic atmos of the Spirit dressing room was automatically transferred to Gosford.

On the field, what I loved was the way he could keep the ball. He had the biggest arse in the club and he knew how to get it between enemy players and the ball. He was a bit unorthodox in his technique but a really intelligent player (and likely to be an excellent coach one day). Also he was one of those players that the fans tend not to notice because he just did his job so efficiently — but coaches notice and so do team mates. He was a really critical part of our early success and I could hardly have been prouder when I was asked to be coach of the Hutch Testimonial team against the Mariners in 2015.

Mind you, I had some difficult times with Hutch. When we were playing Celtic at the Philips International Soccer Sevens in Hong Kong in 2005, Nigel Boogaard had the flu but said he was right to play. Against my better judgment, because I desperately wanted to beat Celtic, I let him play and he was total shite. When I gave him a bollocking for yet another mistake, Hutch yells at me to get off his back because he was sick. So naturally I did the only reasonable thing — I took Hutch off. As he's walking over to the sideline we're both ripping strips off each other and I told him to fuck off to the change room.

Next game was against Man U and he started on the bench and was shitting himself that he might be sent home. After 10 minutes I decided we needed an impact so I sent him out and he made the difference. That win over Man U — despite being against their reserves in a summer tournament — made international headlines. All was forgiven and Hutch was definitely one of the very best for me.

One I've not yet mentioned was young Maty Ryan. He was only 17 and playing for Blacktown when John Crawley told me he was good enough as a back-up keeper to Jess Vanstrattan, but almost as soon as we signed him, Jess got injured and we were faced with the prospect of signing another senior keeper or trusting a kid. I think it was Arnie's very first game in charge that Maty was given his chance and he didnae start well. On a rainy night he dropped the ball at a striker's feet for a tap in, but Arnie persisted with him and it paid off in spades. By the end of his first season he was regarded as one of the best in the league and very likely to be a Socceroo, despite being on the shortish side for a professional keeper.

All sorts of clubs started making enquiries about him and, once again, one of those clubs was Rangers. They definitely wanted him but that was when they were relegated for insolvency and they werenae allowed to sign new players. They would've taken him as soon as they were allowed but Bozza came out in the press and said he shouldnae be going to Scotland – especially not to play in a lower division – so that killed that. Maty, of course, went on to Club Brugge where he was best keeper in the league two years running and earnt a transfer to Valencia. He's also rock solid at the back for the Socceroos and likely to be for another decade.

In an interesting sideline to my discussions with Maty over his potential transfer to Rangers I asked him how he qualified for a British work permit and he said his mum was from Scotland.

'Where in Scotland?' I asked him

'Kilmarnock,' he said.

If she'd not emigrated he could've played for the mighty Killie!

• • •

But without a shadow of a doubt, my greatest success story was Mile Jedinak. The hair rises on the back of my neck just thinking about what that boy's achieved and I couldnae be prouder that I got to help him on his way.

Back in 2006, I got a phone call from an old mate Nick Vravac, a board member from Sydney Utd (where I'd been assistant to Davie Mitchell). Nick said to me: 'Lawrie ... you've got to have a look at Mile.'

'Who the fuck's Mile?'* I asked, but I knew Nick to be a good judge so was prepared to listen.

'He's got the ability to play at any level,' said Nick, 'but he's a bit shy. Will you give him at least three training sessions to see if he'll come out of his shell and show you what he's got?'

So I invited young Mile along for a few training runs and it has to be said — he didnae set the world on fire. But he was certainly competent, so I invited him to keep coming. He wisnae being paid for it and, in fact, it was costing him. He had to drive up from Western Sydney for every session and was still working as a builder, for his old man, John — also a board member at Sydney Utd.

Very slowly, young Mile started to impress me. He was big and fearless — strong in the tackle and good in the air. He also had rockets in his boots when it came to shooting but there was no room in the squad. I would've had to let someone else go to make room for him and that's not my style. So Mile kept paying his own way to train and I think he was fairly close to packing it in to concentrate on building. He probably reached his lowest ebb when we took him up to Toowoomba to play in a pre-season game against the Roar. The night before the

---

* Or 'Mike', as he's known to Tony Abbott.

Mile Jedinak – no-one worked harder to get to the top.
(Photo courtesy Cam Wheeler Photography)

match, we're out for our usual post-dinner stroll and Mile approached me and said: 'Gaffer … I don't feel too good.'

Next day he was so sick he couldnae even go to the game and had to stay in the motel until we came back to collect him for the flight home. I could tell he was very low and obviously thought he'd missed his chance. But his chance did come just a few weeks later when I needed to sign a short term injury replacement. I rang Mile and said: 'Are you ready to play?' and he made his A-League debut against Newcastle.

Before the game I said to him: 'I believe in you, Big Man. You're not gaunny be judged on just one game so enjoy yourself. Win the ball and pass it to one of our blokes … like you do at training.'

Well, that's exactly what he did. He had a steady game in a very demanding position and in particular I remember his ball winning abilities. You'd think the ball was past him but then his legs would shoot out like Inspector Gadget and somehow we'd be back in possession. Lyall Gorman said to me after the game that he wisnae impressed, but I disagreed. I kept playing him and, just like he did at training, Mile slowly came out of his shell and by the end of that first season had not only become a fixture in the team, he was dominating the midfield in every game.

The following season he was on a full contract and had a proper pre-season for the first time as a professional. I think his dad was still expecting him to pack it in and become a builder but 2007-08 was a watershed year for young Mile Jedinak. He was one of the best midfielders in the League, scoring a couple of goals along the way — including an absolute bomb from distance. He also made his Socceroos debut in a team picked by Pim Verbeek, who was notoriously dismissive of A-Leaguers.

His third season was his last for the Mariners. He was once again dominating the league and had scored six goals in fifteen games when his agent, Leo Karis, broke the news: there was an offer in for Mile to go to Glencerbirligi in the Turkish league.

Good news for Mile but devastating for me. In December we were sitting third on the table and playing good football, but Mile was the key to it all. He'd become the glue that held the team together —

everything was built around him — and I knew we'd struggle if he left. But you can't hold back ambition in a salary-capped league. Mile had cost us nothing and had given a lot. It was therefore only fair that we recognised his contribution by standing aside and letting him chase the dream in the big leagues of Europe.

Mile, to his credit, was pretty upset about leaving the team in the lurch, but the door had opened for him and he had to take his chance. While the Mariners received about $800k transfer fee, it scuppered our season. We barely limped across the line into the semis and didnae trouble the statisticians after that. And yet the team was still overjoyed for Mile.

Mind you, he found it very hard to establish himself in Turkey. Shortly after he arrived there was the dreaded 'change of coach' situation. Mile found himself frozen out and was sent on loan to a small club, Antalyaspor, where he played well enough to be invited back to Glencerbirligi, but by then was a free agent. He spoke to Rangers and was offered a contract but, like Wilko, knocked them back. I think he thought it might be a mistake, as a Catholic, signing for such a famously Protestant club. Even so … a second of my players had knocked back the club of my boyhood dreams and it was doing my head in!

Eventually Mile signed for Crystal Palace in the English Championship and we've all watched on in pride as he became captain and then led them into the Premier League. He succeeded Lucas Neill as Socceroo captain and has led Australia in a World Cup and then lifted the Asian Cup in January 2015. For his next trick he led Crystal Palace out at Wembley for the 2016 FA Cup Final against Manchester United, which was truly hair on the back of the neck time for me. Lifting the FA Cup would have to be close to the most cherished daydream of any young footballer and Mile was only 12 minutes away from doing exactly that …

He didnae get to lift the Cup but what he's achieved in ten years is an absolute inspiration to any young bloke out there who wants to be a professional footballer. If you want it bad enough and are prepared to put in the hard work, there's every chance you'll get there in the end.

13

May You Be Fated to Live in Interesting Times

While General Manager of Football at the Mariners Lawrie was not really expecting to coach again, but life can throw up the odd surprise every now and then. To his astonishment, he was approached by the last club on earth he expected to come knocking on his door — Chengdu Blades in the Chinese Super League. Happily settled on the Central Coast and enjoying life in his senior managerial role — did he really want to swap that for the tracksuit and the training pitch in a strange and inscrutable country?

I've heard it said that English, if spoken loudly and slowly, is universally understood.

Well maybe it's my accent, but I was rarely understood in China, and I certainly never understood them. And yet, we did manage to play some decent football from time to time. Mind you, the extent to which good football was down to my coaching will forever remain a mystery because it seemed to me that there were all sorts of influences on games in China, and not many of them could be controlled by a foreign coach. There were strange traditions, hidden and conflicting loyalties, business arrangements, family arrangements and the machinations of money in its infinite forms. And all of this further complicated by the multi-layered subtlety of the Chinese psyche.

I know what you're thinking, but it's not corruption … it's far more complicated than that.

• • •

Seventh insight into coaching

One of my consistent objectives over the years, with every team I've coached, is to establish a winning mentality. A winner's mentality will get you out of situations sometimes where mere skill, fitness, strategy and hard work can't.

I was filling in for a six-vs-six game at training in Chongquin. It was a cold, wet, miserable day and the session was just about over, but with the score tied I busted a gut to get to the far post, slid over the hard icy surface and just got my toe in to score the winner.

The team were all laughing but I picked myself up and said (through my interpreter): 'What the fuck are you laughing for? A 51-year-old has just scored the winner against a team of so-called professionals! Where's your pride? Where's your desperation to win every single contest? You just saw what a 51-year-old was prepared to do to win, and that's what I expect from my team … practice match or fucking Cup Final!'

I think they took my point on board but sometimes a point can be made too well. My first pre-season game as coach of Chengdu Blades was like a scene from a Jackie Chan movie.

• • •

I'd been there a couple of weeks by the time we laced up a boot in anger — and I do mean anger. This came as a bit of a surprise because the Chinese boys were always very polite and considerate. I had a few familiar faces in the team from the A-League — Adam Kwasnik, John Hutchinson, Brendan Santalab and Jonah Salley — which helped me ease into my work, but everyone went out of their way to make me (and Christine) feel very welcome. Everyone except for the club president, of course — he was in gaol for match fixing.

Chengdu was the smallest club in the league with the smallest budget, a state of affairs to which I was well accustomed. But things were looking pretty good in pre-season training, so it was with some confidence that we went into the first game against the local 1st division team.

It seems that despite the difference in league status there was a fairly serious rivalry. Everyone knew there'd be trouble, except me.

The game started placidly enough, but on 23 minutes my polite and humble Chinese boys went completely berserk. It all started from a simple enough handbags situation after a bad tackle, but somehow escalated into World War III. The Aussie boys wandered over to me standing bewildered on the edge of my technical area and stood there scratching their heads. Everybody else was kung fu fighting and it went on for about ten minutes until the game was finally abandoned.

Only one thought was going through my head — the usual thought when changing countries for football reasons: 'What the fuck have I done?'

• • •

Life settled down to comparative normality after that. We trained, we played, and gradually the smallest club in the league found its feet. We were sitting comfortably mid-table and getting some encouraging results, although I was a little concerned with depth. The youth team were stone motherless and didn't appear to have any players worth nurturing into the first team, so I was dependent on the Aussie boys and the best Chinese boys to stay fit.

Now, something which had been bubbling away in the background emerged. The local government had (apparently) promised the club ¥20 million (about $3 million Australian) but hadnae coughed up. I'd not been bothered with it as all my focus was on the team and they seemed happy enough, but one night I was woken at about 1.00 am in my quarters at the training base and summoned to an emergency meeting.

Meetings in China can be quite confusing to simple Western minds — especially secret emergency meetings. They also tend to go through two distinct phases, which I was yet to learn. The first phase is where the Chinese in authority put their heads together and agree on what will be decided at the subsequent 'official' meeting — to which Muggins had just been summoned, scratching his balls and blinking sleep from his eyes.

They explained to me that it was important to put pressure on the local government in order to get their ¥20 million, and the best way to put pressure on the government was to immediately put the ten Chinese players in the first team squad on the transfer list. They presented me with a document authorising the listing of ten players and I thought okay, players get transfer listed all the time without leaving. Can't do any real harm, so I signed the document and went back to bed.

The next morning, there was a very weird vibe about the place. I was trying to work out what was afoot but there was just this depressed silence instead of the usual buzz at breakfast. Then, when we got out on the training pitch, there were ten players missing — the ten on the transfer list. (They weren't entirely missing — they'd been sent away to train by themselves but were effectively gone.)

Immediately I went hunting for the general manager to ask where they were. He explained that they had all been sacked in accordance with my wishes. Seven of the ten had already been sent away and the other three were packing. I was fucking furious. I'd let them talk me into agreeing to the transfer listing but nothing had been said about letting the players go. This was all about the club's fight with the local government.

'We're doing well, for fuck's sake! Who gives a shit about the money when we're mid-table and playing decent football!'

The general manager was adamant that we had to send a message to the government. It was a loss of face to just meekly ignore the insult of not paying up. The only rational response was to destroy the team so the fans would get pissed off and let the government know of their displeasure.

If I thought that was bizarro world, it was about to get much worse.

• • •

The government didnae respond to the sacking of the players, so the club decided to exert even stronger pressure. The big derby was coming up against Xian but instead of the usual one hour flight, the club announced that we were going on a 15-hour train journey. And of course, with ten first team players gone I had no choice but to call up the kids, who were still bottom of the Youth League.

That 15-hour train ride in hot, squalid dog boxes with shite food and hundreds of smokers was pure torture and by some distance the worst preparation I've ever had for any game at any level. The atmosphere on the train was like the middle of a bushfire — hot and smoky — and I remember Adam Kwasnik sleeping on a pile of kitbags, covered in sweat and wheezing like an 80-year-old. And to make matters worse, we arrived at Xian very late and rushed from the train station to the ground just in time to avoid a forfeit.

As I surveyed my motley assortment of Aussie journeymen and Chinese kids — all suffering after our sleepless and toxic journey — I slowly became aware of this strange noise coming from the crowd. It turns out that Jonah Salley had previously been a crowd favourite in Xian, and despite the fact that he was turning out for Chengdu, the Xian crowd — 33,000 strong — were all chanting: 'Salley ... Salley ... Salley.' When we went out for our warm up they would have lifted the roof, if there'd been one. I've never seen support like that for an opposition player ... only in China.

Well, their friendliness didnae last.

Before we went back out for the kick off, I made one of my great Churchillian speeches (which must lose something in translation when you have to wait for the interpreters to do their job every couple of sentences), but I made a deal with the players and said if they gave their all, I'd sing them a victory song. They were all inspired for that in a way that European or Australian players never would be, as it turned out. A mood seemed to come over the team and sometimes you can just tell that the team is up for it.

After all our problems with sacking players and having to get to the game by cattle train, and despite our communication issues and using kids I'd hardly even spoken to in the past, we've somehow managed to achieve the impossible and score a goal. After being pumped the whole game, Kwas got through one on one, completely miss-hit his shot but it managed bobble into the net. As he's standing there arms raised in celebration the rest of the team get down on hands and knees pretending to be train carriages. So Kwas joined the end of the choo-choo conga line. A very fitting celebration under the circumstances.

However, we still had twenty minutes to hold out, and immediately the pressure was on the referee to find reasons to penalise us. The intimidation of the away coach was also beyond what I was used to in the A-League. Even the Newcastle Jets Squadron would have drawn the line at throwing bottles at me. Probably. But not Xian. Great chunks of glass were whizzing past my head but neither the referee nor any other match officials were bothered. Xian had chance after chance but the Chengdu lads managed to hang on and when the fulltime whistle blew it was, without doubt, one of the greatest achievements of my coaching career.

Mind you, we still had to get home, and there was the small matter of leaving the stadium. The Xian crowd werenae pleased with the result and bottles rained down on my lads as they're running off the pitch. The murderous mood didnae let up and we had to get to the airport, but before that the team insisted on hearing me sing a song, so in the middle of all the chaos I was singing a slightly altered version of the Rangers' *Follow Follow*:

There's not a team like the Chengdu Blades
No not one and there never shall be one
Xian know all about their troubles
We will fight till the day is done
'Cause there's not a team like the Chengdu Blades etc

I was *gieing it laldy* and the boys were all grinning and clapping along despite the angry murderous din from outside. The police said we had to go and they escorted us to the bus and that's where they left us. We were into a sea of furious Xian supporters who start smashing and rocking the bus and immediately I felt transported back to my youth when the same thing happened in Turin with the Red Brigade terrorists. The Chinese were worse. Bricks and bottles were smashing through the windows but I was shouting abuse back at the bastards and getting hauled back by the team officials

We were allowed to fly back (thank fuck) and arrived in Chengdu to a rapturous reception from our own fans. In fact, I expected the club management to be pissed off we'd won. I suspected that winning the game in such difficult circumstances would undermine their desire to send desperate messages to the government. But they werenae bothered. The team had suffered miserably, which was all that was necessary to make their point. Everyone was happy.

Mind you, it did occur to me later that nothing could ever be taken at face value in China in those days. What looked like a noble effort against impossible odds, for all I know, was not exactly kosher. And the match really was a perfect candidate for fixing — we had no chance, so the bookies would have made an absolute killing when we won.

Best not to think about it.

• • •

I did witness at least one instance of very questionable behaviour in China — although I suspect that misguided loyalty rather than money was at the heart of it.

We were doing really well in the league. We got a draw away against the champions, Shandong and the following week we were playing Dalian. One of my central defenders was from Dalian and a pretty strange bloke — even by rural Chinese standards. I couldnae easily learn all their names so I had my own names for the players and this mumpty-looking bloke answered to Sourface (if he'd known what his name meant it would have been even sourer). Most players will be fairly attentive when you're talking to them (even through a translator) about their place in the team but Sourface would never meet my eye.

Anyway, against Dalian, we're leading 1 - 0 with about 20 to go and all of a sudden Sourface, who'd played strongly to that point, starts making the most elementary mistakes: passing the ball straight to their strikers, falling over instead of heading the ball when there's no-one near him. And with ten to go and no subs left, he suddenly falls squealing to the ground having 'done' his hamstring. He has to come off, of course, leaving us a man down to survive the last ten minutes.

The very next day I went to see the doctor, expecting to be told that Sourface would be out for at least a month. Instead, I see him

Getting my message across in China. I could have used this bloke in council meetings.

The Great Wall of China was nowt compared with the Great Wall of Aberdeen.

celebrating with the general manager after signing a contract extension. What on earth are we doing extending the contract of an injured player I'm wondering? The answer soon became apparent. He wisnae injured. Sourface trained fully that day — there was nothing wrong with the bastard. He simply didnae want to win against his home town so had done all he could (after we scored) to try and square the ledger.

There was a lot of that in China, players doing favours for friends and family. It's not seen as cheating or match fixing — there's a weird sense of honour about it, but it makes coaching difficult, having to know who comes from where and who's mates with who before you select a team.

I know they're trying to do something about corruption and in 2012 some 20-odd match officials were gaoled. Some of the referees were so bad you'd swear they were sponsored by gaming companies. Substantially cleaned up, there's no argument that the Chinese league has improved out of sight in a few short years and with all the money pouring into the game is likely to improve a lot more. They've dominated the Asian Champions' League for the last few years, but it will be interesting to see how well they can translate club success built on foreign talent into international success built on home-grown talent.

It may take a while but I expect China to be a world football power within a generation.

• • •

Lawrie and the Jets

He's got some football boots

He's quite hirsute

You know I read it in a website ezine, oh, oh, ooooh

Lawrie's at the Jets

Some years after he finished in China, Lawrie learned to his surprise and delight that China was not quite finished with him.

As the great Scottish philosopher Francis Begbie once said: 'It disnae cost anything to have manners. No having them but ... that's cost many a fucker.'

In other words, it's nice to be nice. It's always been my natural tendency to make friends anywhere I go and I find that people are mostly friendly and willing to engage if you show that you are. It's a mystery to me how some people can get through life without accumulating friends, but different strokes and all that.

Even if you only did it for purely selfish or business-related reasons it pays to treat other people well and deal with them honestly. And sometimes the payoff can come years later and totally out of the blue ...

Towards the end of my last term as mayor and long after I'd finished coaching in China, I got a phone call from Rocky (a Chinese football agent with whom I'd become quite friendly) who said: 'I've got someone interested in buying an A-League club ... who's available?'

I told him the Mariners and the Jets were both potentially available and what I estimated the purchase prices to be. So Rocky went away to talk to his people. They turned out to be the LEDMAN Group, owned by Chinese billionaire Martin Lee who already had some extensive football interests around the world and was building a football empire that was neatly integrated with his commercial interests — a really impressive model. Rocky came back to tell me they were definitely interested and asked me to facilitate all the requisite meetings with Mariners, Jets and the FFA as well as with Tony Rallis to discuss a potential third Sydney team.

A week or so later I met Rocky at FFA headquarters with Martin Lee and we had some very positive talks with David Gallup and Damian De Bohun — mainly about taking over the Jets. Then we went off to talk with Tony Rallis about the possibility of setting up a third Sydney team, even though we already knew this was not FFA's preference.

Funnily enough, in the middle of conversations in a posh restaurant, Tony and Rocky started talking about Trent Sainsbury — Tony was Trent's agent and Rocky was a massive admirer. Tony had an offer from a Chinese team for X dollars and Rocky said he could get him double that. While I was out having a piss, Tony called me from inside the restaurant and asked if Rocky was for real. I said: 'Aye, he's a no bullshit straight talker.' So the next thing I know the deal was done and a month or so later Trent moved to China for a jaw dropping amount of money.

But I digress.

I set up another meeting with Paul Lederer, owner of the Wanderers, John Tsatsimas and Tony Popovic to talk about their (stunningly successful) experience in buying a club, which also seemed to give Martin Lee a bit more confidence in the A-League and its possibilities.

The next day we all went up to Newcastle to meet David Eland who was head of Northern NSW Football and in a caretaker role for the Jets. He gave a really strong presentation on the club and then we inspected the stadium. They were very impressed, as they should be, as Hunter Stadium is a fantastic football ground.

I was pleased at how smoothly all this was going but also a little sad as my history and natural connection with the Coast meant I'd have preferred this very serious investor to be dealing with the Mariners. If Martin really did buy an A-League club it was likely to turn out very well indeed for that club, but when we met Shaun Mielekamp — CEO of the Mariners — it was quickly apparent that Mike Charlesworth didnae want to sell, so any negotiated price for the Mariners would be beyond what Martin wanted to pay.

Martin's entourage left the country to think about it and talk to their full board. A week later Rocky contacted me to say they were still interested. I was doing all this just as a favour — putting people together as I'd done my whole career — but you could have knocked me down with a feather when they said that, if they bought the Jets, they wanted me to be CEO!

My first thought was: what do I know about running a football club?

My second thought was: just about everything, really.

I knew the football side of things inside out having been a player, coach and general manager of football operations. I knew how to lead a large organisation — and read a balance sheet — after four years as mayor. What more was there to know?

I therefore accepted with great alacrity and was really excited at the challenge. From that time I became more deeply involved in the negotiations and due diligence and went back and forward several times between Australia and China to help put all the building blocks of the deal in place. At the time of writing (June 2016) the deal is just about done and already seems to have crept out into internet rumour land.

Understandably there's a little bit of negativity on the Jets supporters' forum — me being a Coastie Gyppo coming to turn their club into a dole-bludgers' trailer park and all that. Some of those same fans would have been among the Rowdies at the southern end of Breakers Stadium back in 94 yelling: 'Ooh..aah … Mack-inn-aah!' whenever I entered the fray …

I dinnae mind. Passion's for the fans after all, not so much for the professionals like coaches, players and CEOs. For them it's a job and they go wherever the opportunities are. The fans tend not to understand that and get upset when they dinnae see their own passion reflected in the words and actions of the professionals representing their club. I'd never claim to have the same passion as the fans — even if I've worked often enough without being paid and even put my own money in to support some clubs and players — but I always try to see the game through their eyes and act accordingly (whenever appropriate). If I am appointed CEO of the Jets I'll be trying to rebuild the community support around the club and involve the fans as much as I reasonably can. That's what worked so well at the Mariners in

It's a long way from journeyman striker to CEO, but I always made the best of the hand I was dealt.

the early years so I don't see why it cannae work at Newcastle.

Hopefully by the time this book hits the shelves we'll have already started to turn things around up there.

14

Changes in the Land Where Nothing Ever Happened

The strange intricacies of Chinese football were an education, but for the real dirty work you need look no further than Australian politics.

After five years as coach of the Mariners and another year or so in other high profile roles with the club, Lawrie's success and infectious enthusiasm had made him a popular fellow on the Central Coast.

Popularity, of course, is the great commodity of politics and it wasn't long before both major parties were sounding him out about running for office — something he resisted, until the time was finally right.

In 2012 I was approached to run for council. Monique Marks (Singo's general manager) asked whether I was interested. I said no. What's a council for? As far as I could tell it was just a bunch of whingers sitting about doing fuck all.

Then Singo approached me himself and said: 'Look, nothing ever happens in Gosford because the council's just a bunch of whingers sitting about doing fuck all. If you get elected it'll be one less dickhead to deal with on council.'

So I looked into it, learned a bit more about how it all worked, how you put a team together to garner support and votes, and eventually said yes. The Central Coast has been really good to me so I was happy to give something back. And God knows nothing much had happened in Gosford for 20 years: no businesses were thriving except for the junkies selling drugs around the train station, and certainly no development worth the name had happened since forever. Gosford was *The Land Where Nothing Ever Happened*.

My first public speech took place in a Lebanese restaurant in Erina. All the candidates had three minutes to convince the Erina chamber of commerce that they were worth supporting. One by one the various contenders got up and made more-or-less the same speech: 'Pick me because I've done X,Y and Z in the past and will do X,Y and Z in the future if given the opportunity etc etc.'

In fact, my prepared notes ran along fairly similar lines, but as I stood up to take my turn I was struck by the certainty that I would be buried by all these other more experienced politicians if I played by their normal rules. So I chucked my notes away and said: 'Thanks for the invitation to speak. I had a big decision to make today … I could either stay home and have sex with my wife or I could come here and launch my political career … but in all honesty I knew I'd never last three minutes at home so here I am.'

That got a great laugh and my confidence soared. I spoke very briefly about being non-aligned with any party and just wanting to help get Gosford moving again, then on two minutes and forty-five seconds I said: 'Look at the time. I told you I widnae last three minutes.'

Huge applause, and I knew I was in the game.

But that was just the beginning. Being elected to local government requires an unbelievable amount of time, effort and organisation. And the position's not even salaried!*

We put together a team consisting of myself and some other people I knew from the community with similar values. Then we got stuck into all the campaigning and logistics in preparation for election day.

My confidence got another boost when we went along to the electoral commission office for the settling of the ballot paper and got pulled out of the hat first. Result! Team McKinna would benefit from any donkey voters and I was pissing myself laughing at the mumpty-faced politicians who were pissed off because they took it so seriously.

Then election day rolled around (and I apologise for all the placards

---

* In my time councillors were paid an annual allowance of $20,000 and the mayor was paid $52,000.

everywhere). I spent most of the day at Davistown, which we won massively. Later we had 60 people back at the stadium for a big party as the results were coming in. It was tremendously exciting and very satisfying to get two out of ten as my running mate Gabby Bowles got up also.

But after the election came the wheeling and dealing for the mayoral position. It was fascinating to listen to what the various candidates had to say about what they, as individuals, would do if elected. I was a bit surprised because my whole career had been about teamwork and eventually it occurred to me that maybe I should be mayor. The more I thought about it the more it seemed like the right thing to do, so two days out I put my hand up. 'You've got no experience,' they all said. I thought that might be a good thing. Five old councillors and five new ones — it was time for change in *The Land Where Nothing Ever Happened*.

The way the councillor numbers worked was like this:

Liberals — 4

Labor — 2

Greens — 1

Independents — 3 (including me and Gabby).

This meant it was Libs versus Labor and Greens, with three independents holding the balance of power. Gabby and I could effectively decide who was to be mayor and if I played my cards right it might just be me. Eventually it was the Libs that fell under the chariot wheels of the McKinna charm, although I steadfastly maintain that I am not aligned with them and never have been in any formal sense. My only desire was to make things happen for Gosford and the best evidence of my non-aligned status is this: I have been asked on several occasions by *both* major parties to stand for state or federal seats.

On the night of the mayoral election, I was in the council chambers for the first ever time. Christine was there, my mum was there, and when the vote was announced they were both crying. It was a pretty stunning result when you think about the journey all the way from The Valley: left school at 15, lace worker, van driver, average player and coach of Rag-arse Rovers to mayor of a large community on the far side of the planet.

The day after I became mayor was the day we settled on our new house. One of my election signs was still stuck in the front yard and as we walked up the path for the first time as owners (with my mum out from Scotland) a kookaburra landed on the sign. Instantly I was overwhelmed by a powerful sense of connection with my father who'd died the previous March. Every time he'd come to Oz he'd loved the kookaburras and always made a big fuss about them. I just know that kookaburra was somehow embodying the spirit of my dad and letting me know he was proud of what I'd achieved.

Shortly afterwards I attended an art show where there was a nice watercolour of three kookas. I had to buy it because it somehow symbolised my parents and me when we came out to Australia. I told this story when I made a speech to open the art show and had tears rolling down my face. I doubt the punters expected such an emotional performance but I've always worn my heart on my sleeve. Whether it's charging at a goalkeeper or opening an art show, I've always given it 110 percent.*

• • •

When I started work, I had a lot of learning to do but if it was hard for me it was just as hard for the people at the council who had to nurse a new mayor with no experience in politics or corporate leadership through those difficult early days.

Of course, being inexperienced and uncommitted to any party meant I had no baggage and, in my opinion, the baggage of the various Liberal and Labor councillors with their ancient feuds and inability to agree on the colour of shite was the main thing holding Gosford back.

Steve Glen was the temporary CEO of the council at that time and

---

* Some idiots will try and tell you that you cannae give more than a 100%. Well maybe they cannae, but professional footballers have known for years that a 110% is possible. Like the boy from *Spinal Tap* with his amp, there're sometimes you just need to find that little bit extra.

I was not the first Scot to come out to Australia and be put in chains,
and I willnae be the last.

he was very helpful, but I only had him for a month. He was eventually replaced by Paul Anderson, a kindred spirit in terms of wanting to get things moving. 'Open for Business' became our motto but it took a long time for the culture to change.

For a start, all the staff at the council would bow their heads in respect and call me Mr Mayor. It was like being back in Scotland in the eighteenth century and it did my head in. One day in the lift when some council officer was averting his gaze and calling me Mr Mayor, or Lord fucking Poobah or the like, I said to him: 'Listen! Have you ever been told to fuck off by a mayor before?'

'No, Mr Mayor.'

'Well, *fuck off* and stop calling me Mr Mayor. My name was Lawrie before I was elected and it's still Lawrie. Huv ye goat that?'

That may seem a bit ignorant or even high-handed but I saw it as symbolic of the cultural change that needed shaking up. Gosford was never gaunny get moving with all the same people doing and saying the same old things in the same old way ... and maybe I was frustrated that day. (Okay ... I'll apologise.)

One part of the learning curve for me though was decision making. When you're a football coach decision making is instantaneous. Not in the council. You want to make the slightest change to any kind of policy or previous decision — good luck. You had to lobby every bastard under the sun and get all these focus groups to contribute to a report for a subcommittee to make recommendations to a full committee about possibly changing a comma on a sign in Woy Woy ...

When I was a coach I tried to see the game as a fan and sometimes deliberately made decisions that might please them. Similarly as mayor I tried to see the council through the eyes of a rate-payer. Why does everything always take so long I'd always wondered? Well, I found out why and did something about it, and I truly hope that when people look back on my tenure as mayor they'll see that I did actually get some things done in *The Land Where Nothing Ever Happened*.

And how did I get things done? Individually you can't do anything because council really does work as a team, if it works at all. It took me a few years but eventually, despite all the egos and entrenched perspectives, I managed to get all of council's noses pointed in more or less the same direction. By 2016 we had some pretty decent momentum.

• • •

Major achievements as mayor

- Waterside development ($234 million)

- Old Union Hotel site development ($170 million)

- A billion dollars worth of DAs approved (not including the Lederer Group's $650 million in the Gosford CBD)

- Many sporting parks seriously upgraded (a fundamental promise from earliest days)

- Turned the council's finances around from $8 million deficit to $36 million surplus in four years

- Protected wetland catchments (Crosslands and others) from development and resisted changes to building heritage status (despite the Greens earnestly believing I was worse than Hitler when it came to conservation)

There was also a major restructure of the council itself. We turned most of the temporary staff into permanent staff which meant they were no longer getting casual rates and the various agencies were cut out of the payroll. It was ridiculous that the council had been paying over the odds for years to all these agency-supplied temporary staff while we were going out the back financially. And my predecessors had just muddled along with their brains in neutral, watching the council bleed money.

Obviously there were some people unhappy with so much change but it was all for the best in terms of getting a moribund, bureaucratic colossus ship shape and moving. Council was like a beached whale, but we got it pushed out into the shallows and swimming happily, until it was harpooned by the state government who didnae think we were fit enough to stand on our own re planning decisions.

Then the forced amalgamation with Wyong was like being bent over a table, but at least they promised to use lube!

Well, that's not how it felt

• • •

Amalgama-geddon

Amalgamation had been on the cards since the word go.

The state government had a longstanding desire to rationalise local government — mainly to save money (they said) but also, I think, to reduce the number of different people they had to deal with on the same issues.

I didnae see how they'd save a lot of money providing all the same services to the people of New South Wales, except by cutting a lot of jobs, which again has implications for service provision. As far as I could see the system wisnae broken, which meant the rationale to change it was either ideological or political.

So a main item on the agenda from my earliest days as mayor was amalgamation with Wyong. I had meetings with Chris Hartcher who said the state government would pay for a study to find out what the punters wanted and what savings could be made. My position was that I'd support it if the community supported it, and as long as there were no forced redundancies among council staff.

Well, the state government didnae move too quickly on their study but the subject wouldnae go away, so in 2015 we had a joint council meeting with Wyong and both councils voted unanimously against amalgamation.

So, end of story you'd reckon, but that's not how it turned out. The issue continued to bubble along in the background, and even though the Wyong mayor, Doug Eaton, had voted against it formally, I was aware that he was always in favour of amalgamation, which complicated matters when dealing with the minister.

The state government then wanted us to pay 25% for a study, Wyong to pay 25%, and they'd pay the rest — even though they said earlier they'd pay for the lot. We refused because we'd already done our own study, which found that the community didnae support amalgamation and that the savings the state claimed were not supported by the evidence.

In the end they didnae need a study. They simply decided to go ahead. The two mayors, deputy mayors and CEOs from Gosford and Wyong met with minister Paul Toole late in 2015 and he told us that councils that supported amalgamation could contribute to the proclamation and would be 'looked after', which I interpreted to mean that we would continue to have some sort of meaningful role.

So, clearly 'looked after' is government code for wiped out without any sort of objection or recourse, because that's what happened.

On Thursday 11th of May, we knew something was cooking but even my darkest fears did not prepare me for the reality. At 12.20 I got a phone call from Tim Hurst, acting chief executive of the local governments department, to tell me that council was now under administration. The administrator was Ian Reynolds with Rob Noble as interim general manager.

'What about the councillors, though?'

'They're gone,' said Tim Hurst. 'Now you're under administration, there are no councillors.'

'Fuck!'

I cleared my desk and went home for an hour to clear my head.

I went to my grandsons' football training and had to tell them they were no longer the mini-mayors, which was really sad. Even sadder was when I went to ring Christine and discovered my entire contacts list had disappeared.

All my emails were gone also.

Then, when I went in the next day to hand over to the administrator, my entrance pass no longer worked so I had to sit there like a pork chop for an hour until the people arrived to let me in. That's when I had the pleasure of handing over my precious mayor mobile and petrol card.

I felt like a criminal the way I was frog-marched out. After how hard I'd worked for the council for the previous four years it was a real slap in the face. We achieved so much, got things moving in Gosford and put a human face onto the council, and to be treated like that … I might go for my holidays in North Korea next year just to relive the feeling.

There were a few tears from the staff. It gets pretty emotional when you work so long with people and I had some great people working for me. Thanks in particular to Ariella, my PA. At least the non-elected people at the council werenae getting shafted.

Yet.

Rob Noble wanted me to sit on some panel or other to maintain a bit of continuity but I wisnae interested. It was best to make a clean break.

But as I've said before, one door closes and another opens.

• • •

Federal Politics — 2013

In terms of popularity, I have to admit that that things were going extremely well and others were taking notice. It's a bit like football — have success in the lower leagues and sooner or later the big clubs come calling.

Craig Thomson — by that time famous for other reasons — asked me out for a coffee and amazed me by asking me to stand for Dobell (Wyong Shire) in the federal parliament as a Labor candidate in the 2013 federal election. So I thought about it and spoke to Deborah O'Neill (Labor member for adjoining Robertson, Gosford shire) who was certain I'd win the seat if I stood. I had numerous meetings with the ALP apparatchiks and I was fairly close to saying yes, when the debacle with Kevin Rudd knifing Julia Gillard happened.

The whole thing seriously put me off so I told them no, and had to keep telling them no because they were fairly persistent. But after I knocked them back, Singo contacted me about Team Central Coast. I met with him and ex-test cricketer Nathan Bracken just a few weeks before the election and we decided to have a go — Nathan in

Dobell and me in Robertson. We knew we couldnae win but thought we could use our preferences to get a better deal for the Coast from whoever we agreed to support.

So the horse trading commenced. We went back and forward to the Liberals and the ALP to see who'd give us the best deal. It really was annoying that we had to go to such lengths to win commitment for funding that these people should have been trying to get themselves if they truly wanted to serve the communities that elected them. We thought the Central Coast had been overlooked for too many years. The trouble with electing people from the big parties is that they just fall into line with their colleagues in Canberra and forget all about the people who put them there. They can also have preselection problems if they stick their heads too far above the party parapet — I reckon Peter Garrett would've had his heart broken trying to fit in with ALP policy ... but I'm rambling.

We kept our cards close to our chest — and had two different sets of

Team Central Coast – political footballers, and one cricketer

How-to-Vote leaflets printed — until three nights before the election when the Libs finally promised to move a government agency to the Coast with at least 300 jobs. When I told Deb O'Neill on the Thursday morning she slammed the phone down after making her feelings very plain. My preferences got Lucy Wicks over the line.

For months after Deb O'Neill just smashed me and Singo in the media and blamed us for everything under the sun, from her non-election to the sinking of the Titanic. In particular she questioned my independence, implying I'd been revealed as a Liberal stooge, when what I was really doing was standing up for the Coast in the only practical way I could. And Lucy Wicks, of course, took credit for the jobs after having to be dragged kicking and screaming to support the idea! In the end, though, the Libs may have won but at the time of writing (June 2016) we're still waiting for those promised jobs.

For some reason, after this, people started to assume I was a Liberal Party sympathiser, including the Liberal Party. They approached me to stand for The Entrance (NSW state parliament) but I was never comfortable with that. If they'd offered me Terrigal, where I live, I might have been interested but they didnae want me for a safe seat. With all the ICAC problems they were having at the time they just wanted my profile to help shore them up in the more borderline seats.

As for the famous sleaze and evil of politics — aye, it exists, and it affects everyone on some level. I'd be lying if I tried to claim I was the only squeaky clean apple in the barrel. We're not allowed to do deals in the council chamber but, with all those conflicting opinions and party perspectives, nothing would ever get done unless we reached an understanding from time to time.

Way of the world.

15

Reflections and Projections: The Dangerous Truth

I'll be 55 when this book gets published — just after half-time in the great game of life.

So how do I feel about it all?

As I said at the very start, I truly believe that my greatest achievement (so far) is to make the best of the hand I was dealt. I never had much in the way of natural gifts — but I certainly did my best with what I had. As a person who's played and coached professionally I've seen countless players with more ability than me fail to make the grade because they didnae have the will or the work ethic to rise above all obstacles. Professional football is a massive privilege. They dinnae just hand out jerseys to everyone so if you really want to get to the top you've got to be prepared for a struggle. Every day. Until you get there.

And then it gets even harder because you can't ever rest on your laurels. Every week there are new kids with the same dream and some will be better than you, so you've got to keep working — physically and mentally — to improve your game and your contribution to the team and club. Some kids will say: 'Oh aye, I know I have to work hard.' But the sad fact is that they don't. They may think they know, but then they cut corners or shirk when they think the coach isnae watching. They'll never make it.

I think one piece of genuinely useful advice I can give is this: never switch off during a game. For every player in every position, at any point in any game, there is always a right place to be. You've always got to be thinking to yourself: am I in the best place to help the team right now? And if you can see a better place you've got to get there ASAP and do whatever needs to be done. This is especially true for strikers because they're the tightest marked. Never stop scheming and never stop moving (unless you're trying to put your marker to sleep before exploding into space at exactly the right moment). ˙

Having said all that, football is essentially a very simple game, but it's complicated by too many brains. If the whole team thinks with just one brain, following a strategy, it is the easiest thing in the world to manoeuvre the ball into a goal scoring opportunity. Trap, pass, move — trap, pass, move — shoot and score. Nothing simpler when everyone's on the same page.

A young player who wants to be a professional has got to master the trap, pass and move bit, but he or she has also got to plug into the team brain. Players who can do that are the ones representative coaches look for because the higher you go in football the more it's about strategy rather than technique. Players who can juggle the ball a thousand times or do 20 Ronaldo step-overs are all very well, but I willnae pick them if they cannae follow instructions.

Representative coaches also look for team players — people who put the team ahead of themselves and will do whatever the coach asks them even if they dinnae like playing in a particular position or style. If the team needs you to play in a particular spot in a particular way, then that's what you do without complaint. By all means ask the coach privately about it to understand what he wants and perhaps give your own opinion about it, but dinnae complain in front of your team mates. That affects team morale and, as I've said before, I willnae suffer dickheads.

But what happens, you may ask, when rep coaches do suffer dickheads? What happens when a talented player keeps getting picked in rep squads, despite being a self-obsessed twat, and graduates to senior football?

The answer is Mario Balotelli. He could have been one of the best players in the world but was so distracted by his own personal universe that he wasted his talent and helped to drag down every team he played for. I wouldn't have had him at the Mariners if you paid me — not even to cut up oranges for half-time.

It's sad to say but the dickheads really have taken over professional football at all levels. That's not to say everyone in professional football is a dickhead — far from it — but the dickhead mentality of everyone looking out for number one instead of putting the team first has infected just about every club in the world. That's why the Leicester City phenomenon is so fascinating. Could we be seeing a reaction there to the obscene wages and arse-licking worship of star players which is the norm at all the big clubs? Claudio Ranieri has made it very clear that the team comes first at Leicester, and the players (none of them big stars before they came to Leicester) have bought into that to the extent that they dinnae want him to spend a lot of money in the 2016/17 off-season in case he brings in dickheads. I can really relate to that after the way we built up the Mariners, in the first few years, at least.

• • •

So, back to my reflections. I did the best with what I had in football, and I think I did the same in politics. Australian politics seems to be mainly made up of two schools (and I dinnae mean parties because you have both types in both parties). There are the Passionates and the Professionals. (There's also Clive Palmer but I've no fuckin' idea how to categorise that rather anomalous chap.)

The Passionates are the ones who deeply believe in a particular cause (or causes) and get into politics to try and make a difference. Of course, the causes they passionately pursue are across a broad spectrum so you've got everyone from Bob Brown to Pauline Hanson in the Passionates, all fighting hard for conflicting causes. I have a lot of respect for such people★ although they can be bloody-minded and obstructive when a lot more could be achieved with a little compromise.

The Professionals are the ones who see politics as a career and play the political game as much (if not more) for personal advancement as to serve the community. Both major parties are full of these creatures and I seriously believe most of them would be just as happy in either party — they just want to play first grade.

★ Respect for the people ... not always for their causes.

I think the problem is that most people interested in politics really do start out with a passion on some level, but then they join a major party and the party takes over. You have to fall in line with the party, especially if you have ambition for office, and to fight your way up the ladder you start doing deals. I dinnae mean corruption, it's more a case of 'You support me on X and then I'll support you on Y'. But one thing leads to another and by the time anyone wins preselection in either of the two main parties they're so compromised by doing deals they've got no room to move on any issue at all. This means they have to either resign, or forget their passions and allow them to be replaced by the party's passions.

But the party hasnae passions except power. The party (both of them) dinnae treat us like an electorate anymore. They treat us like a market and we get poked and prodded and surveyed and sampled to see what makes us tick and that's how they formulate policy. Oh aye, they give lip service sometimes to the traditional philosophies of their rank and file, but the actual decisions of both parties in government are nearly always about pragmatism and staying in power. The instant a leader starts to let themselves be driven by doctrine or personal passion the party panics and drives them out. Am I right Tony Abbott? And you know the score, don't you Malcolm?

That's why we need some independents in politics — people who are genuinely passionate about particular issues or communities and not beholden to party politics and deal-making. I saw myself as far more of a Passionate than a Professional but about halfway along the Brown-Hanson Spectrum. I was passionate about getting Gosford and the Central Coast moving — open for business — but I certainly had to learn the professional game or I'd never have achieved anything.

• • •

I've said a lot so far about myself, this being my biography and all, but I've not said a lot about my family, apart from Christine's appalling behaviour from time to time — like the time she was hunkers in the bunkers at Hampden '78 when Rangers beat Aberdeen 2 - 1 in the Cup Final. We were just getting into the ground when Christine desperately needed to go, and it was hard enough to find the Gents'

Four generations of McKinnas.

The love
of my
life.

at Hampden, let alone the Ladies'. Anyway, she spotted some old coal bunkers on the way in and scurried up to find a secret spot. We're all waiting below when a suspicious copper happens along and demands to know what we're doing. 'Erm … my fiancee's just having a pee up there as there's no toilet for girls.'

The bobby's eyes widened and he went straight up to check, then comes back looking a little red-faced and goes on his way. But he wisnae as red-faced as Christine when she comes out shortly after and indignantly complains that a member of the constabulary had been standing there watching her go.

'And how did he even know I was there?' she demanded.

'He must have heard you,' I said. That didnae go down at all well, but she's always been a sport, Christine — the love of my life who has put up with me for 40 years despite having to share me most of that time.

It can be very difficult for a spouse when their other half is a public figure. Even a comparatively minor one like an SPL footballer, A-League football coach or a mayor has calls upon them that are way beyond the norm and it can be trying for a wife or husband who just wants a normal life as a normal couple. They say the divorce statistics are far higher than average when one partner is a celebrity and it's commonly assumed the celebrity is the one who wants away after tasting the illicit fruits of their fame, but that's not always the case. I reckon just as many such couples would break up simply because the other half gets sick of having to share their partner with a world that they are not truly part of. At the very least, the different worlds certainly put pressure on a couple and can slowly drive a wedge between them. You've got to be on the lookout for that and find some time together whenever you can. Holidays help.

Christine, to her credit, usually takes it all with good grace, but it gets wearing. Sometimes when we're walking through Erina Fair (the biggest single level shopping centre in the world) and people are all looking at us and pointing us out, she'll say: 'Have you got your fuckin' horns on today?'

My boys, Scott and Stuart, also missed out on having a normal father because I was away so much both with football and my work as a sporting goods salesman, which put food on the table through all the lean years. I get on with them well now and we've been blessed with some beautiful grandchildren (the former mini-mayors of Gosford), but it would have been nice to have shared more of their childhood.

As for my own childhood: on the one hand it seems like it was on a different planet (Scotland in the 60s), but on the other hand it also feels as though I've never entirely left it. Football and politics are just games, after all, and I've been very fortunate to play for as long as I have.

I've also been fortunate to live most of my life in Australia. Scotland is a beautiful country, steeped in history, culture and wonderful traditions, like haggis and whisky and Mel Gibson's victory over the English at Stirling Bridge. I can carry all that in my heart wherever I go because the Scots these days (like the Irish, Italians, Greeks and Balkans) are an emigrant race. We've spread across the entire globe and made huge contributions wherever we've settled and I like to think I've made a contribution to Australia, the land that took me in and gave me so many wonderful opportunities.

Strangely enough they think I sound Aussie whenever I'm back in Scotland but in Australia there're still folk who dinnae understand a fuckin' word I say. On the one hand I cannae win, but on the other hand I think I've got the best of both worlds. And, it has to be said, the whole thing's gone tremendously well so far.

From Lawrie's Mates: Tributes & Reflections

Jim 'Coby' Cockburn, Kilmarnock team mate

A quote from Rabbie Burns, another famous Ayrshire man, sums Lawrie McKinna up for me: 'Dare to be honest and fear no labour.'

That quote is the boy/man I knew in Scotland and still to this day in Australia, a big honest guy with no qualms about working hard at anything you put before him. You just need to read Lawrie's CV in Wikipedia, it makes me so proud to see what my pal has achieved in the past 30 years, going from an unknown guy playing local football with Darvel to playing with a top team in Scotland and teams in Australia, then onto football management in the NSL, and then he wins the coach of the year in his 1st season as head coach. Then he is appointed into the manager's post at Central Coast Mariners in the A-League and this takes him to another level. Is this too much for this guy? No, he actually takes it all in his stride with Lawrie going onto become the inaugural A-League coach of the year.

One of Lawrie's greatest attributes is he is a people person, that how as the manager of CCM he got the local community involved with the club and the club involved with the community. Its not rocket science by any means but it was as good for the Central Coast people as it was for the Mariner's — coaching from football stars and getting to meet your heroes, as well as getting more fans into home games.

Here is where it gets interesting. Lawrie contacts me to inform me he is going into local politics with a view to getting voted into local council. Not a problem, I tell him, you'll get elected because people love you and respect you in that area. Well, he gets elected the Mayor of Gosford and there I am thinking of him emulating another famous

Ayrshire man, Andrew Fisher from Crosshouse, Kilmarnock — the 5th Prime Minister of Australia. I was actually losing it thinking of how well my big pal has done in Australia.

Lawrie has always displayed a high degree of integrity, responsibility, and ambition. He is definitely a leader rather than a follower. In addition to his excellent accomplishments, he has proven to be an honest, reliable, hardworking and conscientious family man and friend. I am one of his biggest fans and promote his life in Australia to all of my friends and family, so much that my family and friends now follow him on twitter. It is with great pleasure that I submit this tribute for my pal Lawrie McKinna.

• • •

Janene McPhee, Matilda

I grew up in a family that was passionate about soccer, with Mum and Dad (Anna and Johnny) fanatical supporters of, and heavily involved with the Box Hill Soccer Club. I was fortunate enough to meet many people across the years and share in many great friendships — none greater than the Lawrie who I often refer to as my big brother, Christine and the boys, Scott and Stuart.

Living in a four-bedroom family home in Wantirna South in Melbourne, Gary and Scott — my two brothers — and I would often have to share a room to accommodate players coming over to continue their soccer career. Mum would often open her heart and the family home to overseas players that had signed a contract to play with her beloved Box Hill Soccer Club, and she was often referred to as their 'Aussie Mum'.

I recall coming home from school one day in May 1986 to see an old Viscount caravan and a 1963 EJ Holden Kingswood with its original wheels, mudflaps and leather bench seats parked in the driveway. This was to be the home and mode of transport for the McKinna family for the next few months while Lawrie played for Box Hill and as they settled into life in Australia.

I recall many a time we would all be out kicking a ball in the front

Janene McPhee played
football like a girl.

yard, believing we were playing in a World Cup final whilet Mum and Christine were enjoying a cuppa in the lounge room praying that there would be no broken windows.

Having played soccer in Victoria since the age of 13, I moved to Sydney to play in the NSW Women's Premier League in 1988-89. A phone call to Lawrie saw me relocate to Sydney and move in with him and Christine in Five Dock, staying with them for the next 12 months. Lawrie, Christine and the boys are like a second family to me so having them there to support me in Sydney was great.

Lawrie was always extremely supportive of women's football. He would often come down and watch me playing for my local club teams (Box Hill & Sydney Olympic) as well as NSW and, where he could, he'd watch any national team games that I was involved in on home soil.

Looking back some 30 years later remembering the old Viscount caravan and the Holden Kingswood parked in our driveway I will always be extremely grateful to Mum for inviting Lawrie, Christine and the boys into our family.

• • •

David Mitchell, Socceroo and coach

I had just arrived back in Australia from 15 years playing overseas and started coaching Sydney Olympic in the old NSL for their last ten games after they had sacked their coach.

For two weeks I was trying to play and coach … not easy.

I got a call out of the blue from Lawrie. He started to tell me a little bit about himself and I suggested we catch up over a coffee and have a chat. Straight away we hit it off.

Lawrie was interested in getting involved in coaching at a higher level as he was coaching in the 2nd division state league at the time. I needed an assistant and so we became a team. We did very well playing some great entertaining football for the last eight games and became good friends very quickly. Together we went on to coach Sydney United and took them to League Champions (Minor Premiers.) Later, Lawrie took to the head coaching gig like a duck to water and his career went from strength to strength, ultimately becoming A League champions (Minor Premiers) with the Mariners.

What you see is what you get with 'Loz', no airs or graces. He shoots from the hip and has the ability to suss people out very quickly. He wears his Scottish heritage with pride but is grateful for the opportunities Australia has given him and his family.

He has always been a devoted husband, father and grandfather. His family are the centre of everything he does.

He has a great sense of humour, never taking himself too seriously, and that was just as well the time we were on our end of season night out after a great year with Sydney United. The boys had told us we were all to be in fancy dress, so I dressed up as Captain Hook and Lawrie was Peter Pan, complete with green tights that showed off his legs like a ballet dancer. We met in a pub in Paddington and as Lawrie and I paused in the doorway the entire bar caught its breath. Then they all burst into laughter. We were the only ones there in fancy dress and with Lawrie looking so elegant in his tights he was quickly the centre of attention in such a famously gay neighbourhood. He had to disappoint quite a lot of boys that night (or as far as I know he did).

Never in a million years did I think he would get into politics. However, it's not surprising that people have warmed to him. He has a natural curiosity about people and what makes them tick. People can sense that he is genuine. No spin, no smoke and mirrors, no political correctness, just good old honest truth.

Loz takes on each new project whole heartedly and therefore makes it a success. In spite of all this success he is one of the most grounded people you could meet. It's hard not to like him.

We worked closely together for five years and from a random phone call out of the blue he has become one of the ten people in the world I trust and know I can depend on.

• • •

Robbie Slater, Socceroo, EPL champion & commentator

I feel like I've known Lawrie forever.

I first encountered Lawrie playing for Heidelberg when I was playing for Sydney United, which seems like another age of the earth. But he certainly made an impression — a big, loud Scottish bastard who always had something to say and always left his mark. Bruises, barked shins, broken teeth and noses — defenders always knew they'd been in a game with Lawrie McKinna and I was perfectly happy to stay up the other end in comparative safety.

And there was no bloody let up! If he wasn't playing for Heidelberg, he'd be playing for APIA or Blacktown City — it felt like we were playing him every week. When I went to Anderlecht in 1989 I half expected him to turn out for Club Brugge!

In all seriousness, although he was a physical player, Lawrie was never a dirty player and I think that showed later in the teams he coached. They always played the game in the right spirit and it's been a pleasure to play against Lawrie, talk about his coaching on the telly and just to know him for the last 30 years.

He is without doubt one of the game's great gentlemen, and I am proud to have been asked to write a tribute for his book.

• • •

Leo Karis, football agent

I had the privilege of meeting Lawrie McKinna in 2004 when he was building the Central Coast Mariners squad ahead of the launch of the A-League.

What struck me immediately was his honest and affable nature. I have been lucky to meet many coaches, some arrogant, others classy, but Lawrie reminded me of one of my favourites, Terry Venables.

I had come to know Venables when he was the Socceroos coach in 1997 and I had reconnected with him two years prior to my meeting with Lawrie, when El Tel was at Leeds. I have met many good people in football but to this day I have not met better than El Tel and Lawrie.

When it came to doing business with Lawrie, the process was very straightforward and transparent. He very quickly understood the inner workings of the salary cap – a rigid wage system football was adopting for the first time in Australia. We agreed terms on a number of players I was representing including Danny Vukovic, Michael Beauchamp, Andre Gumprecht, Tom Pondeljak, and later Mile Jedinak.

After Lawrie's phenomenal success in the first season, other clubs were circling. What I found extraordinary was that he did not have a contract with the Mariners. Lawrie had agreed to help set up the club, build a team, work for a period of several months for no pay, all on a handshake with Lyall Gorman. And after that stunning first season and a grand final appearance, Lawrie was uncontracted? Really?

Around this time I received a call from Walter Bugno, the Chairman of Sydney FC who was in the market for a new coach after championship winning Pierre Littbarski refused to return to Sydney on a significantly reduced salary. Lawrie and I were invited to a top secret meeting at Bugno's luxury seaside apartment in Dover Heights.

Word had got out that Lawrie was not only the heart and soul of the Mariners, but also the commercial guru bringing in sponsorship money and the club's best ambassador who would visit schools, shopping centres and even attend young fans' birthday parties with several of his players in tow. Over the years Lawrie became known by local media and fundraisers as the go-to-man for charitable causes and the man who would do anything to help the local community. The Central Coast's local hero!

Back on the stools in the Bugno kitchen, Lawrie and I listened to Walter's pitch. He tabled a multi-year offer and we left to contemplate the future.

But news of Lawrie possibly joining Sydney FC somehow reached Gorman who quickly informed John Singleton, a Central Coast resident and Mariners investor, as well as a FFA Board member at the time. Lawrie had struck up a friendship with Singleton and he wasn't about to let his man leave for Sydney FC.

The next evening I had been invited to a meeting with a very influential football powerbroker who was also on the Board of Sydney FC. We were interrupted by a phone call that forced him to leave the room. On the other end of the phone was FFA Chairman Frank Lowy, who declared that the pursuit of Lawrie McKinna was officially over. Singleton reminded Lowy as a shareholder in Sydney FC that it was not appropriate for this deal to go ahead.

The chase for Lawrie McKinna had reached the highest levels of Australian football. What ensued was a meeting with Gorman, which resulted in Lawrie signing a five year contract with the Mariners several days later — a length of contract unheard of in Australian football. And his achievements at the Mariners were phenomenal. On a modest player budget, with limited resources and infrastructure, he was always able to compete and play attractive, attacking football. He was a great developer of young players and the culture that exists at the club to this day has the McKinna fingerprints all over it.

It was no surprise to me that the major political parties pursued Lawrie after his time at the Mariners ended. They knew he had cut through and the punters trusted him. Lawrie's enormous self-belief and his ability to reinvent himself, rising to be a successful mayor of Gosford is truly impressive.

As I wrap up my thoughts, I am trying to think of at least one bad experience I have had with Lawrie. After much deliberation the only thing I can come up with is that it was near impossible to understand the thick Scottish accent on the phone when he was driving on the M1!

Mr McKinna — a true gentleman!

• • •

Adam Kwasnik, CCM player

I have been fortunate enough to have known Lawrie since I was ten years old. Since day one he has been a huge part of my life, not only through football but life in general acting as coach, manager, mentor and mate.

I have shared some wonderful moments with Lawrie and Christine, from them offering my first professional contract to spending daily life in China with them. Through tough times, Lawrie has always been there to offer advice, work through things as a footballer and give me opportunities in life through work before and after my football career.

There have been a few funny moments looking back. In China when we were told we would be taking a 15-hour train trip before an away game it was hilarious. The gaffer was explaining it to us Aussies but he sounds more Scottish when he's angry and wasn't able to get the message across to the Chinese players, who were probably wondering what he was so pissed off about. Eventually he got the translator to explain the problem to the Chinese boys, much to their dismay, but it brought the squad a little closer together.

I remember also the gaffer giving me the opportunity to earn a little extra money working in the delivery business he and his sons had going. One afternoon I had to drive one of the trucks to training at Blacktown and I smashed into a parked car. I was shitting myself thinking what the gaffer would say, plus the fact that I was going to be running late to training. I can laugh about it now (and I didn't get in as much trouble as I initially thought) but that just tells you what a great bloke he is.

I never got the opportunity to watch Lawrie play football but I know he had a distinguished career. Since then, everything he has done has been a massive success. From professional coach to being the mayor of Gosford he always put the players and people ahead of himself. He always gave the players what they needed and he always got the best out of them. As the mayor of Gosford, Lawrie has provided so much for the people and really put that region on the world map.

Throughout the long years I have known Lawrie, I have learnt so much from him in every aspect of life. He along with my father and grandfather have been the greatest influences of my career. In my eyes, he is a true leader and regardless of the situation he has found himself in, Lawrie has always remained a class act.

• • •

Tony Rallis, football agent

How does one begin to describe Lawrie McKinna?

Having known the man for over two decades it became very clear to me in more recent times what a larger than life personality Lawrie really is — a larrikin, an entertainer, a leader, and above all a decent bloke, are some of the initial thoughts that come to my mind.

Whether it was being a footballer in the old NSL with Heidelberg United FC and Apia Leichardt FC, launching and running a successful Mariners FC on the smell of an oily rag or turning the deficit into a profit at Gosford Council. Lawrie did so with a smile, a laugh, hard work and, above all, honour.

You see, Lawrie is a doer and the reason he has been so successful is that he keeps things simple and direct. A man's man that doesn't need an Oxford dictionary to impress, neither does he need to peddle bullshit to make a point. Whether in football, business or politics Lawrie has taken on problems that seemed insurmountable yet succeeded simply because he had people's trust.

In recent years it dawned on me when I spent some time with him in the surroundings of his beloved Central Coast that Lawrie was truly respected for his leadership and vision within his community. Having met some politicians in my time I had never met one that was so respected and, above all, loved like Lawrie.

• • •

Dean Heffernan, CCM player

I first met Lawrie to talk about the possibly of playing for the Mariners back in 2004. Little did I know how much of an impact he would have on my life and football career.

I was playing in the state league for Marconi at the time and during a game for them I could hear someone in the crowd heckling me about my haircut. I had a quick glance over and sure enough it was my new A-league boss, Lawrie McKinna.

I learnt pretty quickly that Lawrie was a very approachable gaffer, but when it was time to work, we worked. That was one of his best qualities in that you always knew where you stood with Lawrie and no matter how good or bad you played or trained, he treated you the same way when you stepped off the pitch.

Lawrie's loyalty and honesty is what made him the gaffer he was, and one thing for sure is that he wouldn't have anyone outside our change room speak badly of his players and club. And if they did he would use it to galvanise us as a group to prove the doubters wrong and show people what he always believed we could achieve.

I am one of the many players he has given opportunities to over the years, and I am always grateful.

· · ·

John Hutchinson, CCM player

When Lawrie first signed for Northern Spirit as the gaffer, I didn't know what to expect. I'd heard a rumour he was a nice bloke so was slightly surprised in the first week when Lawrie told me I had two weeks to pull my head in or fuck off. That's how the relationship kicked off and, to be fair to the man, he was very consistent — he told me to fuck off for the next seven years.

When we weren't getting paid at Spirit he fed us, and when we were playing shit we knew all about it. And when he was happy with us it was always the big Scottish arm around your shoulders and that booming voice telling you, well done, son.

Could anyone else have started up the Mariners and put up with all the crap that he had to? No way.

First pre-season we went to Hong Kong to play in the 7's. We were playing against Celtic in a group game and Lawrie, being a proud Rangers man, was pumped for the occasion. Didn't help that Ian Ferguson (ex-Rangers legend) was sitting next to him. When the half-time whistle went Lawrie was charging towards me, as we had exchanged a few words during the first half. Next I know Lawrie is in my face, destroying me, and then I was in a taxi on my way back to the hotel as the team finished the game off. The next day I got to play, off the bench though. Wasn't the first or last time we had words but it was just the ups and downs of a fantastic manager/player relationship.

Lawrie was passionate and a brilliant man manager and every player that has ever played for him always said the same. Every player would run through a brick wall for him.

• • •

Matt Crowell, CCM player

I first met Lawrie when he invited me for a trial with the Central Coast Mariners back in June 2009. My first session was at Wadalba sports centre and I felt at home straight away. The group of lads he had at the time were the best group I have ever been involved with and that was entirely down to him. You could see straight away that he had respect from all the players and he had a unique bond with every one of them. It was really special to see. Everyone bought into the group and everyone bought into him.

Lawrie has this unique quality of making you feel special all the time, even when he doesn't play you for four weeks on the bounce! His man management skills were the best I've come across and his work ethic was there for everyone to see.

He created the culture that the Mariners stand for today and he's embedded in the club and its history. Still today when you see him at match days everyone wants to speak to him and have photos. He has time for anyone whether it's his number one player or the cleaner at the stadium, he treats everyone with the same respect.

Lawrie helped me settle on the Central Coast and I couldn't be more grateful for what he has done for me personally. I wouldn't be where I am today if it wasn't for the help from the gaffer.

• • •

Ernie Merrick OAM, NSL & A-League coach

I was introduced to Lawrie McKinna soon after he arrived in Australia although I struggled to understand what he was saying as his accent was so broad that he completely annihilated the English language — a true Scot.

Coincidentally we are both from Ayrshire in Scotland and Lawrie had played for the local professional first division club, Kilmarnock FC, before emigrating to Australia. We were both taught physical education by the same teacher, our hero and a legendary player at Kilmarnock FC — Jim McFadzean.

My first impression of Lawrie was of a warm, friendly, gregarious person who enjoyed a crack and a laugh — an auld style football bloke who was a fair competitive adversary on the park and happy to join you for a beer afterwards in the sheds. This, of course, was prior to the introduction of sports science and the adoption of anti-social practices by zealots.

So it was with some surprise that when I coached Preston SC against Heidelberg SC in the old National Soccer League in 1986 that this centre forward (the breed before 'strikers' were introduced) was a fierce, hard-nosed, no-prisoners type of player. I discovered that I had misjudged this Ayrshire gentleman!

Fast forward a few years to 2005, the Hyundai A-League commenced and we became regular adversaries as head coaches of Victory and the Mariners. On one occasion we were interviewed jointly on television and the TV station felt compelled to add subtitles to the production to assist with communication to their audience.

Few football fans, other than those of the Mariners, would realise that as head coach of CCM Lawrie won a Premier's Plate and his team competed in two Grand Finals. He was always a coach with strong convictions and an incredible ability to get the best out of his players. We had many terrific battles on the field and we still have a beer off the field (just don't tell the scientists).

Lawrie is a high achiever and a good person. He is always helping others and it was no surprise to see him become a social leader in the community and the Mayor of Gosford. I don't know what he will achieve next but he has no boundaries — a true Scot.

•　•　•

John McGarry, journalist, *Daily Mail*, Scotland

It's by no means uncommon for Scots to head Down Under in search of a new beginning and a bit of sunshine on their backs. But when I first spoke with Lawrie over the telephone about ten years ago, I sensed immediately that this was not your average ex-pat.

Researching a piece on Scots who were managing football clubs overseas for my newspaper, he relayed to me his fascinating life story which really began to twist and turn the minute he decided to give up playing part-time for Kilmarnock, pack his bags and apprehensively take that 24-hour flight.

Having spent a year in Australia myself, the names of the clubs he initially played for — Heidelberg United and Blacktown City, as I recall — were of huge interest to me. But it was his ability to not just subsequently move into coaching but to reach to pinnacle of the game in Australia that really impressed me. Knowledge of the game is one thing, being a leader is quite another.

For anyone to be named manager of the year in any country is a fabulous thing. For it to happen to someone from overseas — as Lawrie was with the Central Coast Mariners in 2006 — was an even more laudable achievement.

After a couple of jobs in China, it seemed entirely fitting that he returned to Gosford to eventually be the club's director of football.

A passionate football man, I must say I never thought he'd leave the game and when he told me he was considering drifting into politics, I privately feared he was biting off more than he could chew. What did I know? To eventually become mayor of the town spoke volumes about his determination, intelligence and ability to get on with people. It's a story that's long deserved a wider audience — a true inspiration for anyone thinking about moving to another country.

And it's not finished yet.

Playing and Coaching Record

Senior career

Years	Team	Apps	Goals
1979-1982	Darvel		
1982--1986	Kilmarnock	87	17
1986	Box Hill		
1987	Heidelberg United	24	7
1988	APIA Leichhardt	25	5
1989-1990	Blacktown City	31	4
1990-1991	Wollongong City	5	0
1991-1993	Blacktown City	39	25
1993-1994	Newcastle Breakers	7	0
1994	Blacktown City	23	7
1995-1997	Hills United		

Teams managed

1992	Blacktown City (asst.)	
1995-1996	Hills United	
1997-1999	Sydney United (asst.)	
1999-2002	Parramatta Power (asst.)	
2002-2004	Northern Spirit	
2005-2010	Central Coast Mariners	
2011	Chengdu Blades	
2011-2012	Chongqing Lifan	

Also by Adrian Deans

Mr Cleansheets

Eric Judd is 39 and his girlfriend wants him to give up playing football. Eric (aka Mr Cleansheets) is a goalkeeping legend at his amateur Sydney club because in his youth he received a letter inviting him to trial with Manchester United. The letter said to 'come when you're ready' — and six days before his 40th birthday, Eric is finally ready.

Inspired by the dying wish of his Uncle Jimmy, Eric travels to England, but does not quite receive the welcome he had hoped for. Instead, he encounters all manner of villains: murderous football hooligans, Irish mafia, dodgy agents, beautiful pop stars, international terrorists and a range of supporting players with any number of overt and hidden agendas.

But he does get to play football.

The ultimate holiday read – a non-stop rollicking yarn that keeps the pages turning, and if you're anything like me, you'll be starting to panic as the pages disappear in your right hand.
Lawrie McKinna, Central Coast Mariners

If you put Lock, Stock & Two Smoking Barrels, the News of the World and Four Four Two into a blender, the result might well be Mr Cleansheets.
Simon Hill, Fox Sports

Adrian Deans is at his best when writing about football.
Dan Silkstone, The Age

Available at all good bookstores
www.adriandeans.com

Also by Adrian Deans

Straight Jacket

Morgen Tanjenz is a lawyer with an overactive sense of justice. His mission in life is to reward the virtuous, punish the ignorant and avenge those who won't avenge themselves. He dispenses justice via his favourite pastime ('life sculpture'), in which he takes an anonymous interest in strangers – pulling strings in the background to change their lives as he thinks they deserve.

But Morgen isn't the only one changing lives in the city. There is a serial killer on the prowl who taunts police in letters to the local rag but, as the body count rises, Detective Sergeant Blacksnake Fowler can hardly focus on the job with so many distractions. His boss hates him, his deputy is trying to undermine him, and the woman he loves is having an affair.

In the cicada-throbbing heat of a Sydney summer, the threads of a strange story tangle together in a wild conclusion no-one will see coming.

Deans has expertly crafted the novel so that Tanjenz's life sculptures seamlessly segue into the crime mystery, contributing high-stake clues to the watertight plot.
Straight Jacket is not only a well-thought-out and exciting crime thriller,
but also hilarious entertainment.
Newtown Review of Books

Deans has a great feel for the relaxed narcissism that oozes from Sydney's professional classes, and the middleclass banality of Sydney's northern suburbs provides a surprisingly good setting for a book about psychopaths and serial killers.
Law Society Journal

The first person narrator is unconventional, hard to sympathise with, and generally unlikeable for most of the book. However, there is something about Deans' writing that makes you want to read more. The novel doesn't let up, going deeper and deeper into the psyche of the narrator, and into the origins of his warped sense of justice.
Crime Fiction Lover

Available at all good bookstores

www.adriandeans.com

Also by Adrian Deans

THEM

Rob Lasseter is the great grandson of a legendary explorer. His prized possession is an old parchment, which is thought to be a map showing the location of the fabulous reef of gold. Unfortunately, there are no points of external reference on the map. The only words are 'You are here', next to an X, but Lasseter doesn't know where X is – he doesn't know where to start looking.

Inspired by the strange disappearance of the White Haired girl, and the receipt of a letter addressed in his own handwriting from a place he had never been, Lasseter (with his friend Miles, who claims to be dead) embarks upon an odyssey into the centre of Australia and has some very strange adventures. Lasseter thinks he is looking for gold, but instead he finds something far more interesting.

The ultimate solipsist journey …
an Australian story of pan-cosmic enormity.

www.reallybluebooks.com

www.adriandeans.com